POTTERY
A Guide to Advanced Techniques

POTTERY

A GUIDE TO ADVANCED TECHNIQUES

DOUG WENSLEY

The Crowood Press

First published in 1995 by
The Crowood Press Ltd
Ramsbury, Marlborough
Wiltshire SN8 2HR

British Library Cataloguing in Publication Data
A catalogue record for this book is available from the British Library.

ISBN 1 85223 781 3

Dedication

To the memory of Lilian & Archibald Wensley and John Wysocky (sen).

Photographs by the author.
Line-drawings by Bob Constant.

Picture credits

Thanks to all those people, including Stephen Brayne, who kindly allowed their photographs to be reproduced in this book.

Typeset by Footnote Graphics, Warminster, Wiltshire
Printed and bound in Great Britain by The Bath Press

Contents

Acknowledgements

I am indebted to the potters featured in the chapter Personal Approaches. Their generosity and co-operation have added an extra dimension: re-inforcing some of the ideas contained in the body of the book and contributing others.

The contributions from Judith Wensley have been invaluable and legion. As a potter she has provided a personal statement and colour illustrations; she has also given generously of her ideas, research and time. She has assisted with illustrations and photography and has word-processed the manuscript. She has been able to suggest improvements, and add pertinent insertions and focus to technical points. In short she has been a tower of strength.

Finally, thanks to Rosie and John, our children, who manage to put up with us in spite of our being potters.

Introduction

The aim of this book is to build on basic pottery skills and to augment those skills. At the outset it should be made clear that I have not invented or developed the ideas outlined herein, but have simply collected and made use of much of the material over the years. Numerous ideas included have been tried and tested by other craftspeople who have generously offered to share their innovative ideas.

One of the most exciting features of contemporary ceramics is the incredible richness and breadth of creative activity. Any casual visit to an exhibition of ceramic work will reveal a wealth of imaginative and innovative thinking, as well as a wide range of technical expertise. Possibilities in ceramics have never been greater, and it almost follows that a participant's enjoyment of the craft has therefore never been greater either. There are no longer any hard and fast rules, craft practices or taboos to hinder your creative endeavours, only the limitations of what is available.

It would seem that today's potters have at their disposal stimuli unknown to previous generations, as well as a rich depository of knowledge gained by past cultures and the creative output of several thousand years, all readily available through our vastly improved systems. Things all began to change with the onset of the Industrial Revolution in the late 18th century.

During and since the Industrial Revolution in the West, arts and crafts movements have been subjected to radical change, this being particularly true of ceramics. Whereas in earlier times those who could afford pottery were supplied by local craftspeople, the introduction of mass-production in depersonalized factories not only took over such outlets, but was also able to increase the desire, and hence the market, for their new wares. These wares usually came cheaper, both in cost and design quality, and the new manufacturers were quick to develop new markets. The cost to

society was arguably twofold: some, if not all of the intrinsic aesthetic value of hand-made pottery was lost in the mass-production processes; and skills unique to the craft were buried and almost lost under a mountain of often very inferior goods. It would take 150 years for a counter-revolutionary to shake things up.

By 1939 a singular figure had emerged on to the UK ceramic scene. After years spent studying the craft in Japan and Korea, Bernard Leach had returned to the UK and had set up a workshop at St Ives in 1920. The unique experience afforded to Leach in the East was in part made possible by a change in cultural attitude there, and in part by the fact that it had become easier by then to travel such vast distances. Oriental pottery had inspired technical refinements and some superficial copying of surface pattern in Europe since the 17th century, but it was Bernard Leach who introduced a genuine understanding of the oriental expression of creative inspirational potting.

With the publication of *A Potter's Book* in 1940, Bernard Leach became recognized as the prime motivation of a pro-studio philosophy. His life and work were soon seen as being instrumental in revitalizing the craft, and he arguably brought about its renaissance as he led by example. It was Leach who championed the move away from sterile, factory-made pottery, often overdesigned and overdecorated with inappropriate and insensitive appendages and patterns. Individuals were again in control of the numerous stages of producing sympathetic, intrinsically pleasing wares reflecting humble processes and materials. In the post-war period, the craft enjoyed an expansion of participant involvement at both professional and amateur level.

The renaissance was largely craft- and tradition-led at the outset, with emphasis on the pleasure in making, owning and using simple, well-designed and well-made objects. However, due to the desire to emulate Leach on the one hand, and also to the constraints of contemporary technology, studio ceramics was apparently getting a little bogged down. The desire to produce work with the characteristics of wood-fired, reduced stoneware tended to promote a range of wares that was predominantly brown or speckled oatmeal; stoneware was the buzz-word, cone 8 the benchmark and reduction the quality kitemark. That is not to say the work was the worse for that, but these were supposed to be the swinging sixties, and some people working at the time found the techniques somewhat restricting. And so started another revolution, this one slower.

In conjunction with ceramic industry chemists, some potters – notably Emmanuel Cooper in the UK – began experimenting with glaze formulae, underglaze colours and body stains which would ultimately extend the colour range at high temperatures. These developments in glaze chemistry and changes in firing processes have since extended the range of possibilities open to the studio potter. In a similar way, production possibilities have been extended or improved greatly over the last fifty years or so. A growth in interest in the craft has seen the establishment of specialist firms catering for these interests. There is little need nowadays to set up a workshop close to a convenient bed of local secondary clay as a whole variety of such clays are readily available from suppliers, already prepared to suit any conceivable use or preference. Neither is a would-be potter restricted by kiln design or the ability of someone to build one. What cannot be purchased over the counter can be designed, built and commissioned to almost any specification by experts who understand the processes involved; much the same applies to any machinery and equipment a studio potter might require.

The co-operation between studio potters and ceramic industry chemists has also produced some significant advances in terms of technique and approach. Although studio-pottery had for many become synonymous with good and mass-production methods had been seen as 'poor', it does not follow inevitably that all hand-made items are of high quality, and it should not be assumed that all mass-produced objects are inferior to their hand-made counterparts. It should be remembered instead that studio and industrial pottery production have always been linked, both by common

Doug Wensley's innovative stoneware torso.

materials and by common techniques. In recent years, students on ceramics courses at all levels have been encouraged to develop skills which might previously have been considered as primarily 'industrial' and therefore inappropriate to studio ceramics. The acquisition of such skills has significantly extended the visual vocabulary of the studio potter and has been positively encouraged. The result has been an enriching of the ceramic experience, as witnessed in the breadth of activity remarked upon earlier.

Studio potters have also benefited considerably from experience and awareness in the industry of health and safety considerations. Until relatively recently, for example, all potters were at risk of lead poisoning. As a result of precautions taken, however, reported cases of lead poisoning in the UK fell from 432 in 1897 to nil in 1944. The development of non-toxic fritted lead facilitating the formulation of safe 'low-sol' glazes has eliminated the need to use raw lead ingredients. Other poisons such as antimony, barium, cadmium, copper, chromium, selenium and zinc are still in use, but our knowledge of them is now much greater and we can therefore take the necessary precautions when we use them.

Coincidentally the growth in awareness of the potential dangers of some pottery materials has been matched by a similar increase in the range of safe materials now available. It is now possible, for example, to obtain reds which do not rely on the use of lead, do not require a reduction atmosphere in the kiln and tolerate high temperatures. Reds obtained by reducing copper oxides are at best fickle and unreliable, and copper's reputation in health and safety terms is, in any case, somewhat tarnished. So it is reassuring to know that some potters suppliers can offer safe and reliable red stains and glazes, most of which are of excellent quality.

Another hazard to the potter is silicosis. When particles of silica are inhaled into the lungs in the form of fine dust they are surrounded by new lung tissue. The silica remains, embedded, blocking lung capillaries and causing the lung to choke up. Awareness in industry again has brought into force regulations in most countries to protect workers against this condition.

For the modern studio potter, basic health and safety measures can be based on common sense. Wherever possible, use damp or wet material; clean, by washing, all tools and machinery; do not wear dirty, clay-encrusted overalls; and wear a face mask when dry-mixing glaze ingredients.

The foregoing could suggest a morass of danger and restriction likely to prohibit or at least restrict ceramic activity. But be reassured by the considerable increase in participants at all levels, who enjoy their involvement in an almost timeless craft which is developing into an exciting 21st-century form of expression largely free of any hidden danger.

— 1 —

Design

Any ceramic piece, whether functional or sculptural, has been conceived and made by someone, the two processes usually but not always carried out by the same person. Large commercial potteries usually employ designers to develop original ideas, artist-craftspeople to explore practical possibilities, a host of skilled craftspeople to produce the end product, and often a team of artists to decorate the wares at an appropriate point in their production process. The lone studio potter, however, has the daunting responsibility for all these specialist areas of work.

The unique satisfaction of controlling every stage of production – a major reason for being a studio potter – is not always entirely understood or appreciated by potential customers. There is a tendency to question the cost of something which appears to have been made in a relatively short time on a wheel, and out of something as cheap as mud. The visible manufacturing process is confused with the total process from conception to realization, the actual making of the piece usually being considered the most important factor, if not the only one, in the production process.

Techniques and processes are seen as the cornerstones of craft production, as they probably are in most areas. But this begs the fundamental question: is a well-made pot a 'good' pot? The answer to this is perhaps not as simple as it might seem, for while it is possible to define 'well made' in universally acceptable terms, the same is not true of 'good'. Pots, which are subjected to traumatic drying and firing processes, will usually only survive if well made, and most people would agree that a house which has survived for several centuries must have been well made. But is such a house also good? At this point I have to admit to the arbitrary choice of 'good'; I might equally have used adjectives such as 'beautiful', 'fine', or 'aesthetically pleasing'. Sometimes, pots can be positively inspirational. Each definition would have

provoked debate or dissension in its own way. Our understanding of what is 'good' is again pretty universal, but when applied to specific objects such as pots, that understanding becomes less clear.

What does seem clear is that pottery production depends on manufacturing skills which in themselves are impressive and involved. Closely linked to these skills, however, are those of conceptualization relating to design – visual and utilitarian – which are difficult to identify and define, and which are often either taken for granted or, worse still, overlooked.

DESIGN CONCEPTS

There are basically two approaches to design: function-led design, where consideration of usage is primary; and form-led design, where appearance of the end product is more important than other factors. In this respect, design factors apply across the spectrum to anything that is man-made. If we look at a simple design brief it should be possible to identify the major factors that need to be taken into account. At the same time, other minor factors will no doubt emerge.

For example, take the design brief: make a container for liquid. What is actually required here? Something to hold, or contain liquid, suggesting a hollow form which has a base or floor with containing walls. It could be a mug, a cup or a bucket – even a reservoir. The brief as written is therefore not sufficiently specific, leaving the designer unclear as to what is actually required if its intended purpose is to be fulfilled. The brief needs to be written with clear objectives. In the normal course of events, a designer-manufacturer is provided with information sufficient to enable the production of the required object. Either the customer wanted a mug or a pond; clearly only one solution is accept-

Fig 1   Simple variations on the conventional teapot form using cane, pulled or moulded handles according to design preference and 'balance'.

able and so it is usual to communicate the exact requirements in a design brief.

One notable exception to this can be seen in the writing of some examination questions or briefs. Where a candidate's imagination and creative potential are involved, a more open-ended brief is often favoured. In the example above, there are no constraints upon the designer-manufacturer in order to encourage the exploration of a wide range of possibilities. The development of solutions to problems identified by individual candidates would be expected here. Research, development and evidence of particular interests and skills would all contribute to the final solution. In such a circumstance one would expect a wide range, both of problems – mug or pond – and solutions – the nature and appearance of the finished piece. In this sort of situation there is almost more emphasis on the form than on the functional aspect of design; the design brief is itself designed to achieve broader effect.

Fortunately, a craft-potter will usually be involved with projects rather more specific than the above, and will be required to address conventional design and production criteria. So, can the original brief be better worded? This obviously depends on what the customer wants.

A container for liquid might, in the ceramic context, be intended as a storage vessel for conveying or consumption purposes. Usually a much more specific title would be used in the brief – mug, jug, teapot and so on. Using the teapot as subject here, we can consider precise function.

What is required of a teapot?

• It has to contain hot liquid – a hole at the top is required through which it can be filled.
• It is required to pour liquid, usually via a spout.
• It has to be picked up, so it requires a handle.
• It could do with a lid to contain heat, to keep out dust and so on.

From experience, if not from the following sketches, we know that there are other factors to be taken into account. Dribbling spouts have been a constant challenge over the years; a spout which exits (pours) before the filling limit of the teapot is

reached is a more obvious factor. A lid that falls off when tea is poured is also undesirable. Numerous solutions to the latter have been offered, including ingenious locking devices built on to the lid and/or rim of the pot, these often borrowed from designs intended for metal teapots. Unfortunately, such lids are usually only short-lived, due to the fragile nature of fired clay and the short memories of many users. Probably one of the more successful lids encountered in hand-made ceramic teapots is

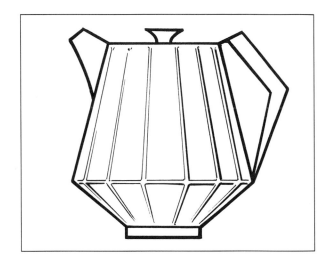

Fig 3 A form suited to metal construction may be less appropriate to ceramics.

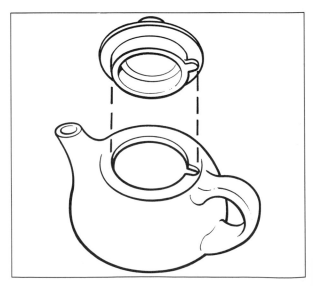

Fig 4 Lid-locking device, easily broken off.

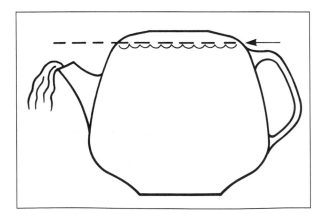

Fig 2 Spout positioned below maximum filling level will cause premature pouring.

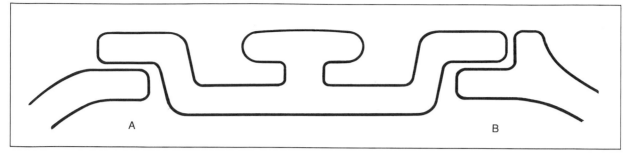

Fig 5 Thrown lid locating either on (a) teapot rim acting as gallery or (b) in a gallery thrown onto the teapot to better receive the lid.

the type where a low centre of gravity is the main contributor to its performance. Further considerations and refinements are suggested in the Teapot project covered in Chapter 4.

Factors Affecting Design

It is likely that designs for a specific item will differ depending on the material selected for its production. Ceramic items have, by their very nature, a different characteristic to similar pieces constructed in metal. And, as construction processes determine yet more characteristics, as seen in beaten, spun or cast metal, so different ceramic processes are reflected in the character of the finished product. Because the form of a piece is to some extent dictated by the method of production, this has to be considered in the design process in conjunction with the choice of material. A hollow ceramic cylinder can, for example, be made by several different methods, each having its merits and peculiar characteristics that need to be taken into account at the design stage. Whether or not a particular process is actually possible will also contribute, if only in a negative way, to the final solution.

Let us look at this in the context of our teapot. If thrown on the wheel, the teapot will inevitably be basically circular in plan at the outset and will look very different from a similar item constructed using flat slabs of clay. There is no reason why either method should be better than the other, and given that equal attention has been paid to the criteria of function, both would work equally well. The major difference would be one of form: the two pieces would look very different and consequently one

might appear more attractive than the other. Such a value judgement is probably more a question of personal preference though, and is likely to differ from person to person. Two completely different processes will produce two articles with very different visual appearances. Both can be equally well made, both are likely to work equally well and both will be attractive to look at, given that the maker has an awareness of design.

DESIGN SKILLS

An awareness of, or instinct for, design is developed over many years in much the same way as production skills are developed and refined. The experienced potter has experimented with many solutions, appearing to achieve finished results with consummate ease. An elegant form thrown on a wheel is always marvellous to witness, and the seemingly casual way in which other craftspeople assemble and build complex sculptural forms is also deceptive. Underpinning these achievements is a wealth of experiment and experience.

One of the things that is not usually obvious to anyone other than the maker is that designs for each piece have been made and considered prior to the start of practical work. Many artists use sketches and working drawings to examine both the overall appearance of the piece and aspects of detail. Others tend to progress empirically, working out solutions as they proceed with the practical work, possibly producing a range of completed items that vary in appearance if not in production process.

Any craftsperson who has made thousands of

teapots over many years will have the dexterity and vision to produce acceptable examples, apparently with ease. Students lacking such in-depth insights will probably need to reflect on details of process and form, and will probably make several false starts on paper or in clay. If initial attempts to produce a particular piece seem unsuccessful, you should not therefore feel disheartened, for everyone has had to make a similarly tentative start. You should also be reassured by the fact that considerable research and development time has usually already been given by others to any problem you may face.

Before moving on from this topic, it seems obvious, but nevertheless necessary, to remind the reader that technical ability will in large measure dictate form. That is, if you cannot command the skills necessary to produce other than rudimentary forms by the chosen means, then time spent drawing complex ideas on paper might be better spent practising. The resulting attempts will provide both expertise in the long run and a range of forms you can actually produce. I have often noticed a correlation between, on the one hand, inexperience and overstatement or overambition in design, and, on the other, experience and simplicity and appropriateness.

The best way forward, therefore, is probably to keep things simple. Certain shapes or forms are more readily made than others, given a particular production method. Obviously, wheel-thrown forms will start out circular in plan. From a side elevation the constraints are likely to be technical.

Keeping Things Simple

Simplifying and 'deconstructing' forms not only assists in ironing out problems of overstatement and overambition, but it also clarifies working and building methods. If a form can be appreciated more simply at the design stage by being considered as a combination of basic shapes, it can probably be made more easily as a result of similar consideration. A simple, tall cylinder can be developed during the throwing process into a form with a fatter 'belly', a waisted neck, or a widened 'lip'. Each stage forms a logical step in the production process, achieved at an appropriate stage so as not to jeopardize the progress already made.

Alternatively, a piece could be conceived and

designed to be made in sections based on the deconstruction of the whole. This would bring the seemingly impossible within the realms of the probable. For example, two bowl shapes attached rim to rim could provide a cylindrical belly form, or tall, elegant cones might provide upper or lower sections for an otherwise impossibly difficult piece. Some of these possibilities will be explored in later sections.

Let us return to the idea of keeping things simple. It can sometimes be helpful to think of pot forms in terms of simple two-dimensional shapes. That is to say, a cylinder is seen as a rectangle, a cone as a triangle and a sphere as a circle. Designing a circle holds no terrors for anyone; it has only one measurement and so will always be the perfect shape. The radius of a circle has a mathematical relationship with its circumference, but size alone is all we have to consider here; proportion does not pertain. A square has only two dimensions: height and width or breadth, both the same. Again, there is no proportion to consider. A rectangle, however, has two different dimensions, so here we are obliged to consider abstract design factors. We are also confronted by the simple, age-old problem which has preoccupied artists and craftspeople, among others, over many centuries. How can a 'perfect' rectangle be constructed? In a mathematical context, how is it possible to produce two dimensions, or lengths, which have a 'perfect' relationship to one another?

Perfect Proportions

A square can variously be described as equal, balanced, perfectly formed, united, symmetrical, or the basis of a mandala symbol. It could also be described as boring. A rectangle, not being a square, could therefore be considered unbalanced, asymmetrical, disunited – or at least less boring than a square. The degree of disunity, inequilibrium or interest thus rests with the relationship of the two dimensions: height/length and width/breadth.

Permutations of height and width are obviously legion. Designing a 'good' rectangle therefore has almost limitless possibilities, and the profile shape and proportion of a ceramic form based on a rectangle will, to an extent at least, also be determined by its use, or function. Nevertheless, convention has determined some rectangular

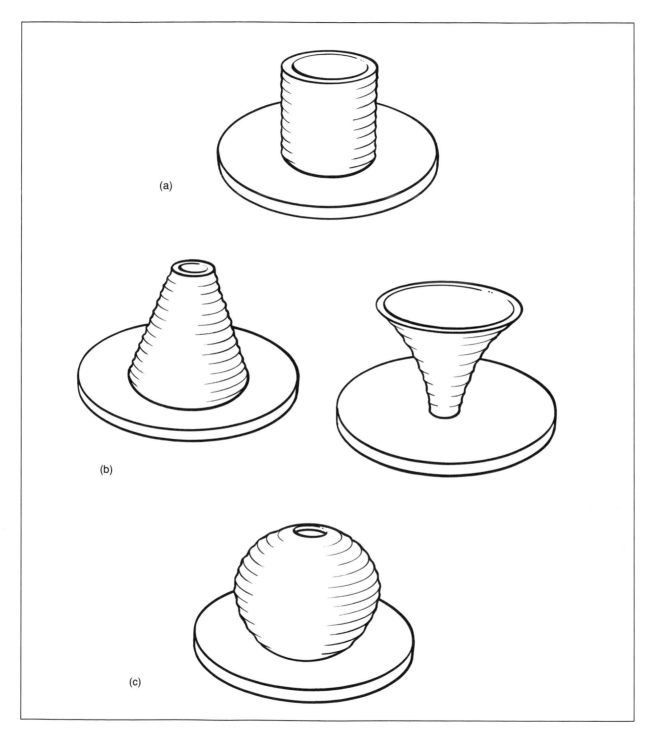

Fig 6 (a) vertical sides are self-supporting; (b) a cone can be stable, earthbound and comparatively easy to throw, or elegantly precarious in appearance and having a tendency to collapse if thrown too thin or into an exaggerated shape; (c) a strong form once thrown, this requires a considered approach plus turning if a very small foot is desirable.

shapes as being 'better', or aesthetically more pleasing in appearance, than others. Paper and book shapes are classic examples of acceptable convention. In the relatively recent past, it was possible to obtain paper in both various sizes and, more significantly, various proportions. Standardization to the 'A' format has to an extent phased out alternatives; photocopiers and PC printers are only designed to work with the new format. The consequent restriction of choice in this respect may be offset by financial convenience; books will fit on the shelves. However, they may still not be everyone's idea of the perfect rectangle.

This elusive relationship of one measurement to another so preoccupied both artists and mathematicians during the pre-Renaissance period that eventually, sometime during the 15th or 16th cen-

turies, a mathematical formula, the Golden Mean Rule, was established to enable the construction of the Golden Mean Rectangle. The extent of the formula's unique beauty is not within the brief of this book, but the recipe for a basic Golden Mean Rectangle can be. Using a ratio of 8:5 as the relationship between height and width, a rather elegant rectangle can be constructed.

If a simple cylinder with proportions 5in (12.5cm) in diameter and 8in (20cm) high is made, the result is a mug-shape which conforms to the Golden Mean Rule. Such a construction has proportions very similar to mass-produced mugs which are widely available as commemorative, tourist, feature or promotional items. The appearance of this particular shape and its subtle variations is obviously popular. It is clearly easy to produce, and relatively

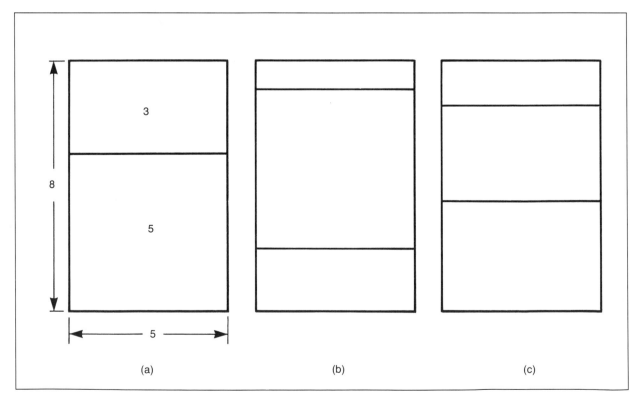

Fig 7 Where one dimension is altered a totally different form can be produced. 'Golden' rectangle/ cylinder (a) simple division into a square plus a 'golden rectangle' based on the ratio 8:5.
(b) The square now divides the rectangular 'balance' into sub-divisions echoing the 8:5 idea.
(c) The 'golden rectangle' subdivides the square according to the 'golden mean'. Decoration of a simple cylinder affords limitless permutations, achieved by banding (painting; oxides, slips, etc), dipping (slip, glaze), or double-dipping. This offers contrasts of glaze/underglazed; rough/smooth; light/dark, etc.

cheap. Its simple, clean shape and proportion is at least neutral; it seems not to offend one's sensibilities. And it is readily decorated using a range of techniques and specialized motifs, including transfer mug strips.

Fig 8 Mug strip using effective division of areas into small graphics area balanced by larger undecorated area.

Varying Dimensions

A rectangle can also have one or other of two formats, as illustrated. When applied to a three-dimensional ceramic form, these two formats result in either a tall or a squat cylinder. The choice of format will depend on both personal preference and intended use. The form with an appended handle could fulfil the function of a mug, but in all probability a similarly handled form of the second type would seem inappropriate in that context.

The important message here is not that there is a uniquely beautiful and mathematically correct rectangle on which to base a cylinder. Rather, there is a huge range of subtle variations which the enquiring potter can explore in the quest for pleasing forms. These variations are likely to develop into the third basic shape, the cone. If the possibilities

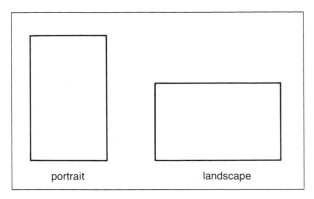

Fig 9 Tall and squat (portrait and landscape) profiles.

of the simple cylinder are extensive and subtle, the possibilities of the cone are limitless.

The reader will readily be able to imagine the implications of having three rather than two variable dimensions with which to experiment. A conical form could either be stable or extremely unstable, totally 'earthbound' or elegant, and re-

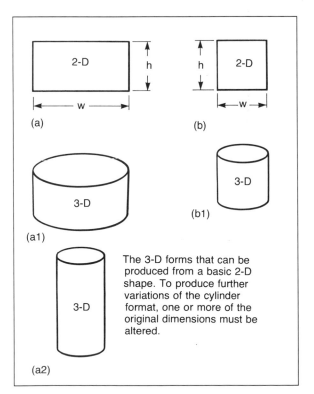

The 3-D forms that can be produced from a basic 2-D shape. To produce further variations of the cylinder format, one or more of the original dimensions must be altered.

Fig 10 Simple variations to the cylinder format.

Fig 11 *By changing one dimension at a time a cone's appearance can be drastically altered.*

fined or absurd. Function can again assist and clarify to some extent; the visual appearance will also depend on aesthetic preference. One person's idea of an elegant jug form may be considered by another to be unstable and therefore completely impractical. A jug blessed with a non-dripping spout might none the less seem unbalanced or 'lumpen' to some users. The aim here, however, is not so much to match form with function as to indicate an approach to developing generally reasonable shapes.

It is possible to restrict activity to the confines of simple, single, geometric forms while still achieving practical pots. Straight, cylindrical mugs, jugs or vases would no doubt 'work', and they might well be attractive in appearance, but a creative potter might consider such constraints tedious. The challenge is more likely to vary, modify and distort these basic shapes, while at the same time allowing them to grow naturally into each other or to combine them to produce a composite whole. As will be found during the process of throwing, some composite forms develop naturally, while others will require encouragement through planning. In other words, it is helpful to know what you are trying to make, and the stages through which the piece has to progress – in other words, how the end is to be achieved. Practical issues relating to the manufacturing process will be clarified through projects illustrated elsewhere in this book.

Developing Your Ideas

Returning to the premise that simplicity is preferable to overstatement and overambition, an ideal

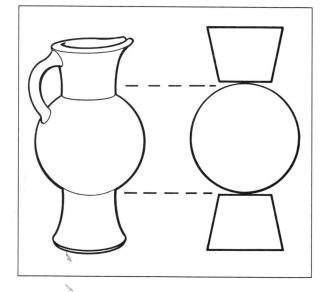

Fig 12 *Deconstruction of traditional jug-form into composite parts; two cones and a sphere.*

way to start developing ideas is to use a sketchbook. Thumb-nail sketches, using profiles based on simple geometric shapes, can be of immense value. A wide range of ideas can be explored quickly and then refined for more detailed consideration. This could lead on to more specific sketches, prototypes produced as part of the selection process, or perhaps a combination of the two approaches. The results will inevitably include interesting variations in shapes, together with indications of how best to proceed in practical terms. Analysis of a sketch will provide a breakdown of component (geometric) parts and, in some cases, an indication of how to prefabricate sections of the proposed piece.

Throughout this book there are examples of how finished pieces can be designed and manufacturing processes planned to best suit assembly requirements. The reader will be encouraged to take full advantage of any creative ideas by working within constraints imposed by technical ability or availability rather than struggling against them. For example, the lack of a potter's wheel or a gas-fired kiln should not be seen as disadvantageous. Instead, make the most of what is possible or available and turn restriction to your advantage. If you cannot meet your objectives then change them, as an old friend of mine once urged. So, if you don't have access to a potter's wheel, or if you cannot actually use one, make the most of the skills you do have and of the tools available to you. There are a number of low-tech methods of making ceramics which will be illustrated in later sections of this book, one or other of which may well prove to be a challenging and rewarding alternative to wheel work.

2

Ceramics and Clay

WHAT IS CERAMICS?

To understand and appreciate the concept of ceramics, it is worth reflecting first on what is meant by the ceramic process. Ceramics (from the Greek, *keramos*, or pottery) refers to the making of objects from clay which is then metamorphosed by fire or intense heat into a new material: the trinity of earth, fire and water.

In fact, our 'earth' is clay which, in its plastic, malleable state, contains free water. As the material dries out this free water is released to the atmosphere, the clay remaining chemically intact; by re-introducing water to the material it can be reconstituted to a workable, plastic state. The crucial change from one material to another is only brought about by the action of heat. This metamorphosis involves the driving off of water chemically bound up in the molecular structure of the clay, resulting in a new material which is hard and porous. This is usually referred to as biscuit or bisque ware. The ceramic nature of an object is simply that: it is made of clay; it is thin (relatively, so that it will withstand thermal shock); and it is fired and transformed by the action of heat.

Background and History

This principle has been understood and utilized much longer than pots have been thrown on some sort of wheel; it has older and stronger traditions which are based on forms of hand-building with clay. Both useful domestic ware and decorative, ritualistic or sculptural pieces have been produced by people throughout the world, and prior to the advent of the potter's wheel these were usually women.

Such hand-built pottery normally reflected vigour and growth associated with nature and the closeness of the maker to it. Forms were natural and grew almost casually to fulfil desired functions. Decoration was direct and reflected the intimate experience of the maker, being influenced by traditional women's occupations of basket weaving and textile manufacture. Motifs were often associated with plant and flower forms, as well as human and animal detail, and again referred to the makers' close association with his or her environment and way of life.

Around 3000BC this ancient tradition of pottery was subjected to its own revolution, both cultural and industrial. The development of the potter's wheel, attributed to the Egyptians, was to have far-reaching effects on the craft. Hitherto, pottery had been produced at a leisurely rate, consisting more or less entirely of one-off pieces made, as mentioned above, by women. The wheel, representing technology and probably developed by a man, became the tool of men. Pots could now be mass-produced, and were usually decorated in a more mechanical manner as it became possible to decorate on to a revolving, circular vessel. Banding was effected, and geometric forms and motifs superseded the gentler, lovingly executed artwork of the more sensitively conceived hand-built pieces.

Modern Views

The production of ceramics in the West has been dominated by the wheel since its development in the Middle East – at least, until now. As observed in the introduction, wheel work as a mass-production process fell into decline as new technology was introduced in the first half of this century. In a sense, the history of the craft has come full circle as we have been freed from the historical dominance of the wheel and from the ignorance of other cultures. We have been given the freedom to challenge rules and conventions; the field is wide open for experiment and innovation. We can make whatever we choose, and are responsible to no one but ourselves.

Since we have returned to the 'original situation', as I tend to call it, and have inherited a vast wealth of technological and historical resources, almost anything, therefore, is possible, subject only to our own creative limitations. How then do we proceed to make something? The original idea might be suggested by function, materials, techniques or processes, imagination, or observation.

• **Function led.** If you start with the idea of producing a useful object such as a jug, you will be constrained to a greater or lesser extent by other factors: the material used; how the material will be used (thrown on a wheel and so on); whether you, the intended maker, actually have the special skills required for the chosen technique.

• **Materials led.** You might start by investigating the potential of the material. Discover what can be done with different clay bodies. Is one clay more suited to a particular form or process than another?

• **Process led.** A hand-slabbed teapot will be very different in appearance and form to a thrown pot. Its character will essentially be 'slabbed', in the same way that an industrially slip-cast pot will have its own character unique to the process.

• **Imagination or observation led.** You might start from the premise that a teapot form, for example, could be based around the theme of transport. Or, by drawing from plant forms, seeds, buds, flower details and the like, ideas could be extracted which lead to a concept for a teapot form.

• **Experimentation.** Experimenting with a number of techniques might prove to be a profitable way of playing your way into an idea or project. At the very least it might let you know that one firing technique affords different effects and properties to another.

In subsequent sections there will be illustrations and examples of some of these alternative approaches. The most obvious factor in our equation is, inevitably, clay. Perhaps it would be useful, therefore, to look at the basic material used in the ceramic process and discuss ways in which it might influence the manufacturing process.

CLAY

Clay is extremely common, and as a raw material it is both easy to find and usually relatively cheap. Its unique property is that it is plastic in its damp, heavy, natural state and it is this property which makes it such a versatile manufacturing material. In this context the term 'plastic' refers to clay's property of being malleable, or capable of being manipulated by numerous means into shapes which can be maintained while the material is still in its plastic state. Moreover, the clay can then be returned to its original shape and formed into something else, providing that it has not been allowed to become dry.

What is Clay

Clay is hydrated silicate of alumina, having a theoretical clay crystal structure with the formula $Al_2O_3.2SiO_2.2H_2O$, and should certainly not be confused with mud. This remarkable material has equally remarkable origins. Clay was at one time either igneous or metamorphic rock which then decomposed slowly. Granite, upon decomposition, first yields silicates, salts and feldspar. This feldspar can further decompose to the end product kaolin(ite), at the same time releasing mica, quartz and further salts and silicates.

In its purest form, mined from the site where it originally decomposed from the parent rock, clay is usually referred to as primary clay. The most important of these residual clays is China clay, noted for its whiteness and purity, but, because of its relatively large particle size, lacking plasticity. Another important primary clay is bentonite, which conversely is extremely fine and plastic.

Due to the ravages of weather and erosion, primary clays can be carried – as a suspension in river water, for example – and deposited well away from the site of the parent rock. Such secondary clays can collect a wide variety of impurities *en route*, these altering their appearance – iron oxide, for example, can add the characteristic terracotta colour to clays such as red marls. As a consequence of these weathering, abrasion, frosting and leaching processes, particle size is broken down to produce finer, more plastic clays. The clays often also pick up discolouring organic matter which causes them to smell, but which burns away in a firing.

Where is Clay Found?

Clay usually lies buried beneath more recent deposits of rock, sand and earth that have been washed down and deposited in caves, river beds and back gardens. Many small local potteries used to rely on clay dug locally, not least because it was impossible to transport such a heavy raw material over any significant distance. The characteristics of local potteries were thus determined to some extent by the characteristics of locally available clay bodies. The Honiton Pottery, for example, was a family business based on a red clay dug from a back garden. In the long run, however, this clay proved unreliable in its properties (colour, shrinkage, resistance to damage in firing and so on), and so more consistent supplies were sought elsewhere.

Some self-reliant potters still seek local clays, and are prepared to work extremely hard to win low-cost material from the ground. Others tend to blend own-brand bodies using raw materials purchased from a supplier; these will possess individual characteristics as required and determined by the individual craftsperson. More often, blended bodies are mass-produced and purchased for a specified purpose.

Clay Properties

As mentioned above, a primary clay is usually 'short' (lacking plasticity) due to its particle size; secondary clays tend to be more plastic. Clays containing significant quantities of sand will also be short, while the blending in of a plastic clay will modify the condition. Fireclays, which are naturally short, can be crushed and blunged to produce extremely plastic clays that reflect their origins as shales or flaky, compacted sedimentary clay.

One of the most plastic clays of all is ball clay. This clay is not usually used on its own because of its excessive plasticity and slippery qualities, but instead is widely used as a major ingredient for blended bodies. Its name refers to the practice of digging such clays from open quarries in handy sized lumps of about 25lb (11kg) called balls. Ball clay is frequently included in glaze recipes to provide adhesion before firing and to help keep the glaze in suspension.

The plasticity of a clay body depends not only on the natural composition of the material but also on the way its minute particles are arranged. When these particles are encouraged to lie in the same plane, lubricated by moisture, the body can stretch and bend readily. But, as after much use and recycling, when the particles are chaotically disarranged, clay can become tired and much less plastic. As we are only on this Earth for a fraction of the time nature has taken to plasticize clay, we can only rest it to an extent. By wedging and kneading, however, and leaving the clay for a period of rest practicable to the user, plastic qualities can be revived. These processes will be referred to in more detail later in this chapter.

What Clay to Use?

In the past, potters had little choice of which clay to use – clays available in the immediate vicinity would have been used, either direct from the ground or blended with other local bodies to improve the characteristics. Where no suitable clay could be found, there would have been no great ceramic activity. Cost would not have been a major factor, for transporting large, very heavy loads was simply impractical. Only limited trade in pure kaolins to provide white bodies would have been possible, and such bodies would have been used sparingly because of their scarcity and cost.

Contemporary students of the craft can almost be forgiven for thinking that clay is a product manufactured in some huge factory complex rather like washing powder. After all, it comes in similarly handy packages, plastic-wrapped with name and catalogue number clearly printed thereon to aid and inform the consumer. And we, as in numerous other consumer areas, have an almost dazzling choice of so-called designer clays. These clays are sometimes far removed from the original quarry site, as any reference to a supplier's catalogue will testify.

Unlike the case of washing powder, however, a uniform product, or choice of uniform products, is entirely justified here: potters need to be able to select clay bodies according to use. Preferences will depend, among other things, on the manufacturing and firing processes, the nature of the glazes proposed, and colour and texture. We are no longer confined to local materials as transport is easy, not excessively expensive, and quick.

Suppliers can make available to us bodies, either from stock or blended to individual requirements. This enables us to spend more time making things and much less time risking back injury and unpredictable results by digging clay from an unreliable source. The advantages of such a system are varied and obvious. In short, we can usually obtain a ready, reliable body to suit our specialist requirements, and this can be reordered on a long-term basis. We can also expect it to be delivered to our door!

However, such convenience does cost, and not just in terms of money. The satisfaction of winning and blending our own bodies has gone, and we have lost touch with one of the more fundamental aspects of the craft – contact with the Earth. It is therefore worth attempting to dig for clay every once in a while as a break from using standard bodies, as a return to basics and as a means of realizing the qualities and potential of what is, after all, the craft's basic raw material.

So, how do you decide which clay to use? Well, it rather depends on who and where you are, or rather how you are involved with ceramics. If you are a student making use of equipment and resources that are determined by the establishment you attend, then there may be no choice. Or you may perhaps find two bodies to hand – red earthenware clay, possibly best suited to the production of press-moulded dishes and smaller thrown pieces, plus a grey, stoneware, throwing body. The latter appears to be the preferred choice of experienced students who extol its virtues in reduction firing, although peer group influence might overshadow practical considerations.

If, on the other hand, you have set up a workshop and have yet to acquire clay, then the choice is yours. Suppliers' catalogues are the obvious place to start, bearing in mind the type of kiln you will be using. If you do not have access to a kiln, then solve that problem first. Returning to the catalogue, select a clay that seems to fit your situation: if you intend throwing all or most of your work and want to stick with earthenware temperatures, then a good, red clay may well be best; if you intend to build very large sculptural pieces, then a heavily grogged grey body such as raku or crank might be more appropriate instead.

There are self-reliant potters who dig local clays, and there are 'others-reliant' potters who 'inherit'

clay. The most important point is that you have some. Just get started, and sort out any preferences you may have as your experience increases. More specific advice will be offered in subsequent sections concerned with the making, decoration and firing of pieces, all of which may feature in the decision-making process.

USING THE RAW MATERIAL

A casual encounter with the raw material – clay – may show it to be in excellent working condition. If this is the case, it will be wonderfully plastic, malleable and totally homogenous. In the hands of an experienced craftsperson such clay will appear to have life, vigour and a desire to adapt itself to the will of the maker in a most co-operative manner.

Conversely, the clay may be either too sticky and unsupportive, or excessively hard and unyielding. As is often experienced in evening classes, for example, the condition of the clay may well suit the needs of some of the group but be less than ideal for others. If the clay seems right for throwing it may well be too soft for hand-building processes and may be extremely difficult to roll out into flat slabs. In an ideal world, clay will be prepared precisely to suit the needs of maker and process, but more usually, the maker has to take responsibility for preparing a clay body appropriately, assuming that its condition is less than perfect when initially encountered.

Throughout the history of pottery, clay has built up a reputation for itself which can sometimes almost be taken as myth. There are stories about potters who dig up clay, prepare it for use, then dig holes in the ground and bury it – perhaps for two or more generations. When resurrected, this clay is found to have impeccable properties, making it much more desirable to work with than a body just recently dug.

If clay is recycled constantly – for example, reused after numerous workings on the wheel – it is said to be tired and in need of a rest. In this state it becomes less plastic, or short, and will be difficult to work. However, if it is prepared, stored properly and then more or less forgotten for weeks or months, tired clay will often revive. A system of rotating recycled clay, allowing periods of rest, can be seen to be beneficial, giving credence to the folklore. A part-time student attending pottery classes only once or twice a week therefore seems to be at the mercy of circumstance, or, in some cases, even mismanagement. So, how is clay treated in an educational establishment?

Nowadays, clay is usually purchased from suppliers in 25lb (11kg) plastic bags, as mentioned in the previous section. It will have been de-aired and prepared in average plastic condition and, on delivery, may not be ideal for a given purpose. The likelihood is that when a new bag of clay is opened it will be rather too stiff. Suppliers do not wish to be accused of selling water, and so have to tread a wary path between introducing too much water and too little moisture content to their products. Clay in plastic bags can, and will, dry out in time. Storage in dry conditions – such as in the same room as a kiln – will shorten that time, while storage in a cool, damp environment conversely can extend the time almost indefinitely. There is no guarantee that clay taken from a newly opened bag will either be suitable for its intended use or be in the same condition as when it left the supplier's premises.

Recycled clay, often referred to as reclaim, will have been soaked down, slopped out to dry out naturally, and probably put through a pug-mill before being stored in a bin or plastic bag; this will usually have been done by a technician, or sometimes by a student. When clay has been pugged it is usually thought to be in working condition, but, as in the case of the new bag of clay, this assumption is based on optimism and faith rather than observation and fact. There will, of course, be occasions when the clay will be exactly right for the proposed job, yet others when it will not. It all depends on what actually went into the machine. Was the clay still a little too soft? Or was it too stiff? What can be done about discrepancies?

Preparing Clay

Preparation is crucial. The traditional methods utilize the following:

- **Nature.** In other words, the clay simply dries out in the atmosphere.
- **Absorbent surfaces.** These absorb moisture from

Fig 13   Using a vertical pugmill to recycle clay.

the clay, and include plaster of paris in the form of kneading slabs and moulds.
- **Hands-on processes.** Kneading and wedging.

If a pug-mill is used some of the harder work can be avoided, as can some of the uncertainty of leaving the process to others – provided, that is, you have free (or supervised) access to a pug-mill.

When clay is just a little too soft (only experience will tell) it can be stiffened by kneading on a plaster slab. This will homogenize it at the same time, and is not too demanding in terms of either effort or time. However, if the amount required is large or if the clay really is excessively soft, the pug-mill can be valuable asset. Use your pug-mill as follows:

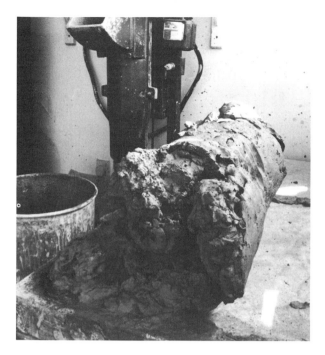

Fig 14 Drying out slops.

Step 1 Have ready the soft clay, plus a small amount of stiffer clay.

Step 2 Add, say, a golf-ball-sized lump of harder clay to a tennis-ball-sized lump of soft clay, and feed the combined lump into the pug-mill.

Step 3 Process the whole batch and check the consistency. It is as well to remember that a large, vertical pug-mill will contain upward of a bag of clay *before* you put yours in, so do not expect the first extrusion to be perfect. Feed in plenty to exclude the original contents and repeat the process as necessary, adding softer or harder (but not dry) clay until the desired consistency is obtained.

Avoid using sloppy, almost liquid clay, or clay that is excessively hard – even the pug-mill will have trouble digesting extremes, and by introducing such clay you may actually make things more difficult in the long run rather than easing the work. Used intelligently, however, the pug-mill will enable you to reconstitute clay either way in relatively short time. Remember, though, that pugging is not

Fig 15 Wedging stiffened slops.

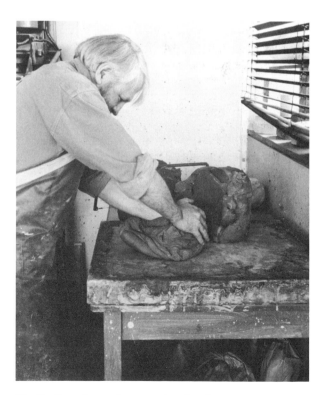

Fig 16 Kneading to homogenize the clay.

a substitute for kneading, this being essential to ensure total de-airing prior to throwing.

ODD PROPERTIES OF CLAY

- Clay does not absorb water readily. Subterranean layers of clay inhibit drainage; ponds lined with clay existed for ages in the days before butyl liners.
- Damp clay is less inclined to absorb water than is completely dry clay.
- Dry clay in small, thin pieces will break down in water more readily than larger lumps. The latter appear soft and slimy on their surfaces, but internally they remain dry.
- Such properties can help or hinder the potter, particularly in recycling clay, or mixing slips or glazes.

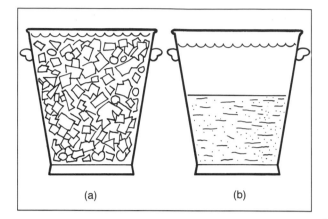

Fig 17 Dustbin of dry reclaim: (a) shards with water covering to soak down; (b) clay 'soak' settles out leaving clear water above to be syphoned off or bailed out.

Recycling Used Clay

It is best to allow 'failures' and waste to dry out completely before adding water. Larger lumps should be broken up prior to soaking – use a hammer to administer sharp, tapping blows. Sterner measures will be called for when attempting to break up solidified bags, whereby the judicious use of a hand-axe can be effective. Compression, by impact, can render lumps both more shock-resistant and less inclined to absorb moisture. The effects of compression will be less on totally dry clay than on slightly damp clay; dry lumps can crack; damp lumps usually do not.

A dustbinful of broken pots and small pieces of dry clay will soak and settle down considerably over a period of time. Due to particle size and content, some bodies will disintegrate more easily than others. Eventually, clay will settle out, leaving water at the surface. This water can then be decanted before slopping out and drying the clay.

As a final note, however, remember that prevention is always better than cure. Avoid the need to replasticize bagged clay by storing it in a cool, damp, frost-free place.

In Your Own Workshop

If you have your own workshop, and hence exclusive rights to preparation systems, some of the foregoing will seem superfluous. You will be able to keep reclamation down to a minimum by kneading small quantities of clay as they build up, and you will be able to mix and soak harder clay with the slurry and trimmings from throwing. There will be little or no completely dry clay to cause hazardous dust, and you will be able automatically to prepare reclaimed clay to your own requirements.

3

Advanced Throwing

It is probable that most experienced potters would prefer to throw blindfold rather than attempt to define the word advanced in this context. Where one person might struggle for an hour or more to throw a modest bowl, another might dash off a dozen in the same time. Meanwhile, someone else's impressively large vases might look amateurish when seen beside another's wonderful little gem of a bowl. In other words, techniques or methods which might appear advanced to some will inevitably appear basic or obvious to others. Nevertheless, two factors seem to impress the layman and novice alike: the ability to produce large thrown wares; and the ability to produce sets of similar looking pots (repetition throwing). Before looking at either of these as an advanced technique or otherwise, however, we should consider the basic element that divides the beginner from the expert. An experienced craftsperson works *with* material and equipment, while the novice often struggles against them. Getting everything right is not finicky; it is to your advantage to have everything prepared or arranged to your liking.

BEFORE YOU START

Preparation

The clay body must be homogenous and of a consistency you can handle. A body that is too stiff will be difficult to centre; very soft clay will 'grow' easily but will be incapable of supporting its own weight in anything other than simple, probably vertical shapes.

Quantity

Students often expect clay to stretch somehow beyond its volume. If large vessels are the aim, sufficient clay must be available (*see* below).

BEFORE YOU START

- Prepare the clay for the job in hand.
- Have enough clay to do the job.
- Recognize the limitations of the material.

Limitations

This relates partially to consistency: a grogged body will support itself more readily than an extremely plastic, smooth body. Porcelain and some smooth earthenware bodies will therefore require rather thick throwing with considerable turning later. Exaggerated shapes will similarly require extra thickness for support prior to stiffening and turning down to the required shape.

Cross-Sections

Where a lump of clay is thrown as in (a) in the diagram below, the cross-section and thickness are adequate. If height is maintained as in (b), but the form is overstretched, it will be prone to collapse.

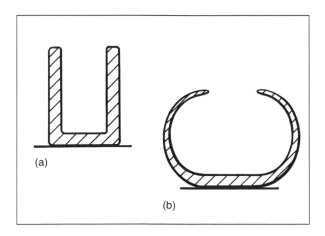

Fig 18 A cylinder (a) overstretched to form a sphere of the same height (b) will be too thin to support itself.

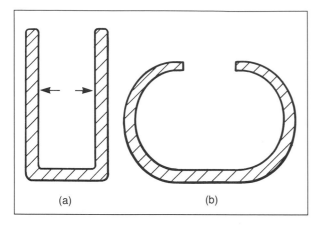

Fig 19 Extra height is necessary to allow for loss as form is widened. To create the sphere apply pressure at the points indicated by the arrows.

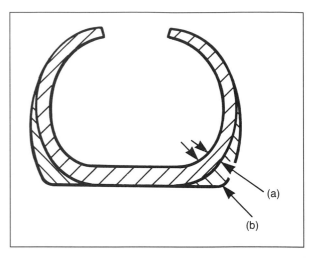

Fig 21 As the clay dries out it will shrink and pull the rim in and down, so allow a little extra height. Leave excess clay (b) to provide support. This will be turned off later to leave (a).

In practice, if a cylinder as in (a) in the diagram above is thrown to a height of 6in (15cm) and the shape subsequently modified to a sphere, the height of the sphere will have been diminished. Watch someone throwing to witness this shrinking of the vessel. So, in order to achieve a 6in-high (15cm-high) sphere, at least 50 per cent more clay would be required.

The above deals with quantity. Limitations imposed by the clay body include collapsing or sagging as in Fig 20. If such a shape could be thrown evenly thin as drawn, it would soon start to sag out of shape. In order to overcome this prob-

Fig 20 The upper section lacks strength to support itself.

lem it would be advisable to thicken the lower parts so that they support the upper sections, and lessen, initially, the inward curve of the lip of the pot. Excess thickness can be turned off when the pot is leather hard.

Turning

Throw a bowl with an overthick base. Allow it to stiffen and, when ready, gauge the thickness in the base and lower walls by measuring (plumb the depth). Measure the walls by gently pinching, with fingers inside and thumb outside the pot, to get a feel of the thicknesses. Use your thumbnail to scratch the outside walls where thickness is excessive. These scratch marks will be turned off later, and deep or shallow scratchings can, to a limited extent, indicate the amount of clay that needs to be removed. With practice, reasonably uniform thickness changes are built into each pot, and with them a better understanding and knowledge of what is required in the way of turning. In short, before turning a pot, get to know it thoroughly.

Bowls can be inverted directly on to a potter's wheel, centred and turned down without problem. Taller pieces will require careful attachment to the wheel-head, and a sensitive application of (sharp) tools to avoid accidentally pushing the piece off-centre and off the wheel-head. Pots with narrow lips, including the spherical example cited above, will need to be supported on the wheel-head in some kind of chuck – it may be possible to make use of an upturned bowl as shown.

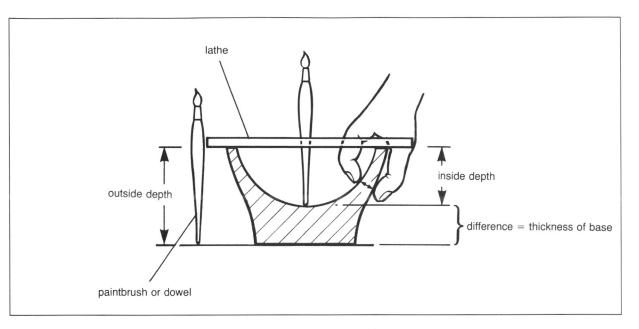

Fig 22   Use finger and thumb to 'feel' the thickness of walls; use brushes or dowel rods to measure inside and outside depths. The difference between inner and outer equals thickness of foot.

Fig 23   Bowl used as a chuck.

Step 1   If necessary, turn the base of the bowl or chuck to ensure level centring.

Step 2   Make absolutely sure that the chuck is properly centred and affixed to the wheel; use soft plugs of clay to stick it in place.

Step 3   Invert the pot into the chuck, and fix it to the rim using soft clay as on the wheel-head if necessary.

Fig 24   Use soft plugs of clay to fix the chuck to the wheelhead.

Fig 25 Turn off excess clay.

Step 4 Turn off excess thickness.
Step 5 Carefully release the pot and chuck, removing the soft pads of clay.

Custom-made chucks can be thrown directly on to the wheel-head, allowed to stiffen, and then used and discarded before they become too firm to re-cycle. If runs of repetition thrown pots are to be turned, a biscuit-fired chuck would be more durable. Other alternatives include plaster-cast and turned chucks, and bought-in chuck heads that fit some potter's wheels, both these probably being inappropriate for most studio potters.

Summary

* Work with the material by having it prepared exactly for the job in hand.
* Avoid handicapping by using inappropriate or insufficient material.
* Do not expect to make a ready-to-use product

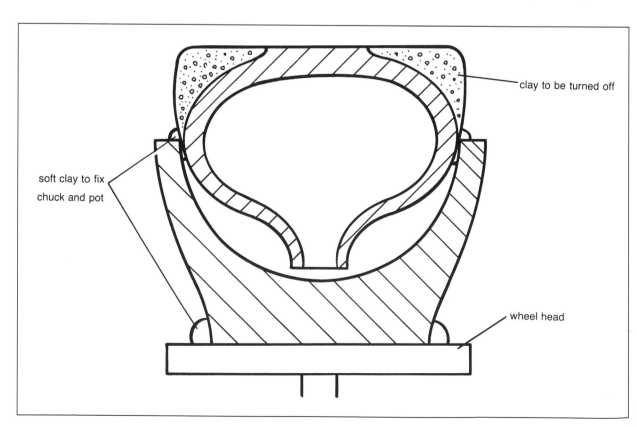

Fig 26 Method of securing a narrow-necked vessel for turning.

without recognizing all the limitations – of the materials, processes and your own abilities. Careful consideration should always be given to the basic properties of clay.

The above example of the production of a spherical form illustrated the need to consider preparation, quantity and limitations. Incidentally, it also made reference to turning and the use of chucks as a means of overcoming one of the limitations.

THROWING LARGE VESSELS

As suggested above, size is determined in part by quantity. The first problem when throwing a large pot is to make up balls of clay that are larger than would normally seem manageable. Psychologically, it seems, larger lumps are somewhat threatening at first. If you find that this is the case, build up in modest steps to start with, developing more confidence as your success increases. Keep to vertical forms in early practice sessions, gradually increasing your repertoire to include wider, more open shapes (such as bowls) or vase shapes.

Learning to Throw

There are probably three ways of learning to throw:

• Watch an experienced potter – endlessly if possible.

• Practise, with an experienced thrower providing one-to-one advice and encouragement.
• Practise on your own until you get it right.

My own inclination is to progress through these points, falling back a stage as necessary. An alternative might be to start by reading appropriate books. As a sole means of acquiring experience, however, this method falls very short of adequate, but a book can none the less offer some unique support. As a starter, reading and examining photographs can provide initial impetus, while the book can also provide a sort of stationary action-replay, allowing the reader to examine at leisure actions which otherwise happen too quickly to be analyzed to any extent. You may also be able to identify solutions to any part of the process that proves to be a stumbling block.

Tall Pieces

Whether it is large or small in real terms, a 'tall' pot has height relative to width. To gain height, clay has to be elevated from the wheelhead. This involves applying pressure inwards and upwards at the base, some of this before the clay has been opened, and (indeed, usually most) after opening but prior to serious shaping. The sequence of photographs (overleaf) illustrates a method of throwing a tall pot, and includes an indication of how to centre and open the clay.

When throwing small and medium-sized lumps of, say, 1–7lb (0.5–3kg) in weight, balls of clay can

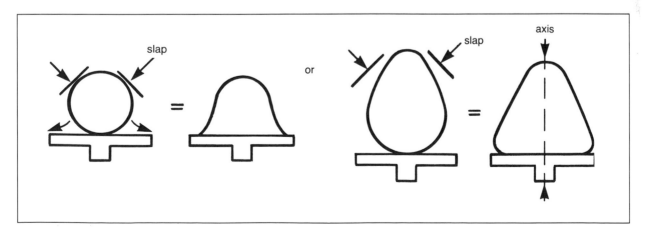

Fig 27 Slapping clay into shape.

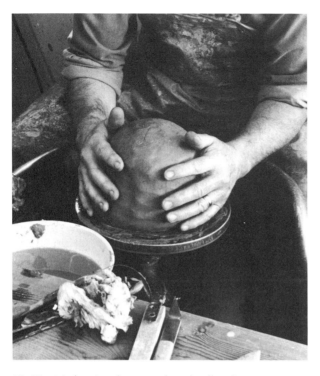

Fig 28 (a) slapping down on the wheelhead.

(b) centring.

(c) punching to open the clay.

(d) or use thumbs to open.

(e) collaring to gain height.

(f) drawing up.

(g) drawing up.

(h) trim off excess from foot.

readily be centred. Either slam the clay firmly down on to a slow-turning dry wheelhead, or place it carefully into position over the centre of the similarly dry wheel, turn it, and simultaneously slap the ball down into a cone shape using both hands.

Larger lumps can be preformed like a pear, and then slapped down. The aim is to centre the mass of clay above the axis of the wheel so that it requires only a minimum of fine tuning once the wheel is set in motion. This reduces the need to fight bumps as they revolve, and so the more centring that can be done by slapping, the less is required by throwing.

Throwing in Stages

The perfect scenario doesn't exist as far as throwing is concerned. That is to say, if the clay is soft enough to centre easily, it might well be too soft to support height and weight; conversely, when it is firm enough to support its own weight it may not be easy, or even possible, to centre the larger amount necessary to achieve the desired height. As in so many situations, a compromise has to be reached.

Compromising with time can be one way forward. Use the soft body to centre, open and collar easily, then when a reasonable start has been made, leave the clay to firm up prior to final shaping and cleaning. This could take considerable time depending on conditions in the workplace, and also ties up a wheel. You can further compromise on sensitivity to material and traditional craftsmanship, speeding up the stiffening process through the application of hot air – use a hair-drier or electric paint-stripper, taking care not to cause uneven drying or to dry the piece too rapidly. If the pot is turned slowly on the wheel and the warm air applied to the areas that need to be stiffened, both inside and out, the piece will soon be ready for further thinning and shaping.

I have found, however, that it is sometimes a good idea to part-throw a piece before lunch, the break being sufficient to enable further work later on. Pots can be left for longer periods, such as overnight, again depending on the working environment. If the piece is partially covered (particularly the upper part) with a plastic bag, the remaining exposed, lower parts will firm up while the upper areas will remain workable. Remember that it has

taken millions of years for the clay to become the plastic material we use today, so an hour or two spent transforming it into something else is as nothing against such a backdrop.

Building as You Throw

An interesting variation on the above method is to throw, say, half a vessel to your maximum height (possibly 14–16in, or 36–41cm), keeping the section reasonably thick.

Allow the piece to stiffen until the top is firm enough to be scored. Apply slip and then a generously proportioned coil of soft clay. Model and/or throw some of the new clay down over the join to ensure really good adhesion, then draw the additional clay upwards to form the next part of the vessel. Add further coils as conditions allow until the vessel is complete.

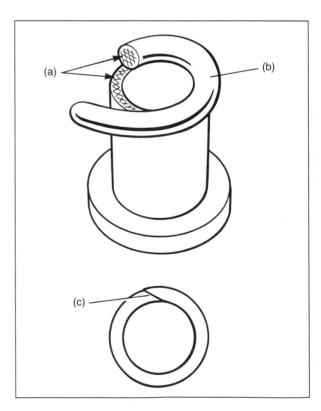

Fig 29 (a) score and slip top of thrown cylinder. (b) add a fat coil or soft extrusion from pug-mill. (c) cut and join at an angle to obtain a stronger join in the added coil. Score and slip join prior to modelling together.

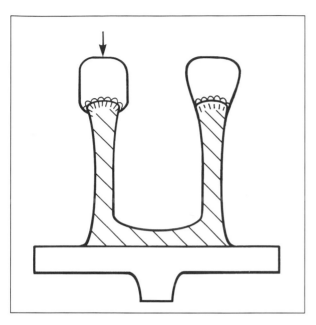

Fig 30   (a) new clay pressed down gently but firmly to weld properly to old clay. Score and slip join prior to modelling together.
(b) restart throwing from just below area of join to stretch and compress clays together.

In order to consolidate and compress the joins, and to disguise the same if desirable, use a wooden rib or metal kidneys inside and out. Turning (when leather hard) will also remove uncomfortable undulations in the profile shape, but be careful not to turn away too much in these areas as joins may become exposed and weakened.

Reassurance – Centring

When centring small lumps of clay it is important to ensure that no wobbles exist. The profile of the centred beehive or solid cylinder shape should appear to have no movement (wobble) as the wheel revolves. With large lumps the accuracy is less critical: a slight wobble at the upper extremities will be thrown out as the piece develops. In fact, if a large lump is opened by punching, the resulting open cylinder will seem decidedly uneven as the clay revolves slowly. As soon as the drawing-up pressures have been applied once or twice, from the bottom upwards, most if not all irregularities will have been evened out.

The ability to manage large lumps on the wheel

Fig 31 (a and b)   Using a rib to compress joins.

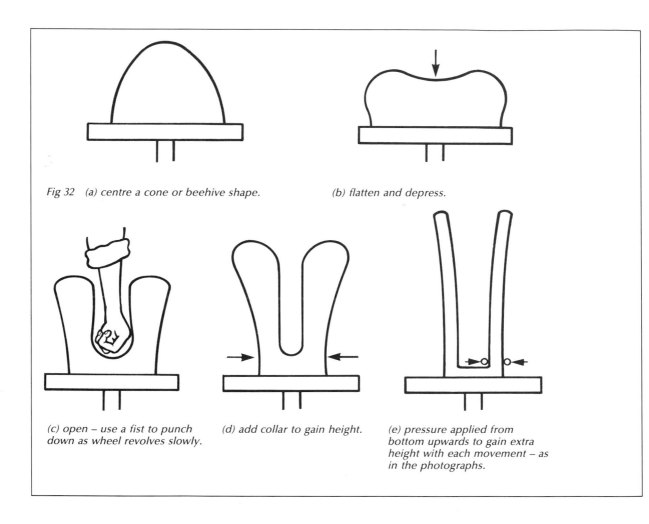

Fig 32 (a) centre a cone or beehive shape.

(b) flatten and depress.

(c) open – use a fist to punch down as wheel revolves slowly.

(d) add collar to gain height.

(e) pressure applied from bottom upwards to gain extra height with each movement – as in the photographs.

comes with practice, and with having or developing confidence in your ability. Remember, you are doing the throwing, the clay is not throwing you!

TIPS

- It is better to have too much, rather than too little clay.
- Concentrate on gaining (early) height – worry about shape later.
- Remember to increase thickness pro rata with height – don't try to throw a pot that is too thin.
- Excess clay can be turned off later; err on the thick side.

REPETITION THROWING

The apparent ability to produce exactly similar wares is an excellent sales pitch. Without doubt, there are craft skills involved, but, as a practising potter yourself, remember that you can actually throw a dozen items or more from which to pick your matching set of half a dozen later on.

A couple of basic factors assist greatly in achieving similar end products. Obviously, starting with the same-sized lumps of clay is necessary. With smaller items such as cereal bowls, accuracy in weighing out is very important – if one ball is 2–3oz (57–85g) heavier than another when the desired weight is only 8–10oz (227–283g), there will be a possible excess of 25 per cent, this being reflected in the eventual size.

To repeat forms successfully it also helps to get into a rhythm. Therefore, plan to throw a reasonable batch, if necessary writing off the odd one or two early attempts made before the rhythm has been achieved.

Mechanical Aids

- Callipers
- Adjustable markers
- A gauge post could be obtained from a pottery supplier. Under most circumstances the gauge post or the DIY alternative will be sufficient, giving a guide to a few basic dimensions without being overly restrictive or forming an incumbrance. Where it is necessary and desirable to produce exact profile repeats, a template can be cut either to aid throwing or to check final turning.
- A more flexible means of achieving a similar end is to use ribs, either from the outside or within the vessel. The advantage of ribbing is that clean, precise profiles are possible. Against this, as with

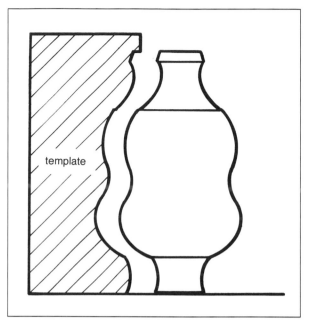

Fig 33 A template can be cut from card, hardboard, etc.

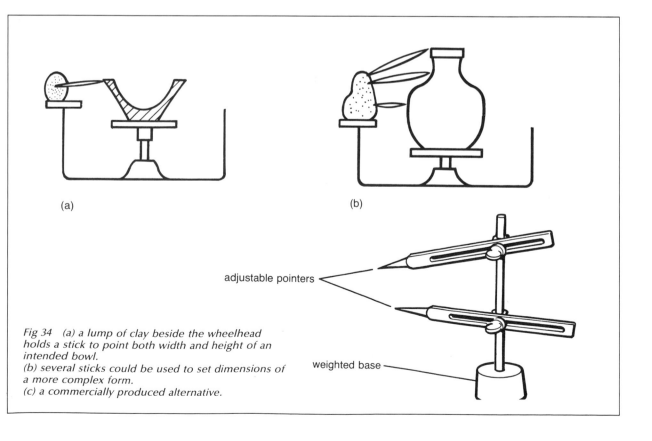

(a)

(b)

adjustable pointers

weighted base

Fig 34 (a) a lump of clay beside the wheelhead holds a stick to point both width and height of an intended bowl.
(b) several sticks could be used to set dimensions of a more complex form.
(c) a commercially produced alternative.

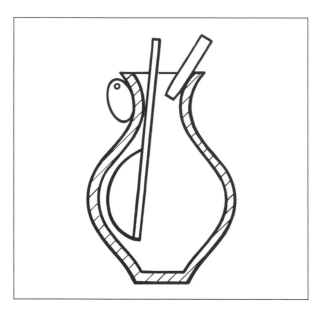

Fig 35   Using a rib to check internal thickness.

excessive turning, throwing marks are removed, lessening the feel of spontaneity and life that is inherent in vigorously thrown vessels.

A comfortable, fence-sitting view of the foregoing is that most studio potters nowadays are only usually required to make repetition runs of simple forms. Mugs, bowls and jugs in modest numbers can be thrown with basic guides, minimum ribbing and turning, and can usually retain much of the vigour of the spontaneously made one-off piece.

Throwing 'Off the Hump'

The centring of small balls of clay (anything less than a couple of pounds in weight) gets progressively more difficult as size diminishes, for it is both easier and quicker to centre one large lump than it is to centre a number of small balls. The idea with throwing off the hump is to capitalize on the convenience of having only one large ball to centre upon the wheel, using only the top of the lump or hump to produce small pots, one after the other. The main mass of clay remains centred firmly on the wheelhead, and only the top part requires reconing after removal of the previous pot. The protuberance at the top of the bump can then be thrown in the usual way.

Fig 36   Throwing off the hump, using callipers to check size.

Finishing and Removing

Pots thrown in this way obviously cannot be removed from the wheel in quite the same way as direct throwing permits. Finish the pot in the usual way, using a sponge and/or chamois inside and out to remove slurry. Turn off any little excess weight, particularly at the foot, using a wooden dog-ear tool and cutting as narrow a foot as is practicable. Cut precisely horizontally to release the pot, using a twisted wire (no water). Lift the piece gently from well in at the foot and place it on a dry board.

This technique is particularly useful for the production of small, open forms such as eggcups, mustard pots and little bowls. It is possible to throw a lid off the same lump as will be used to throw the body of its parent jar or teapot. It is also possible to throw a series of lids, knobs or spouts, again without the need to centre more than one piece of clay.

Fig 37 Removing a small bowl – note the twisted wire marks repeated on foot.

Fig 38 A spout thrown off the hump.

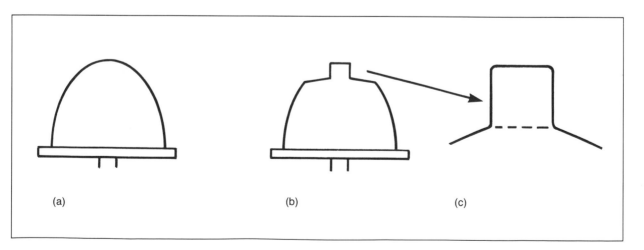

Fig 39 Off the hump: (a) centre a large 'beehive'; (b) throw a small solid cylinder at its top; (c) top cylinder replaces the alternative small ball centred directly on the wheelhead.

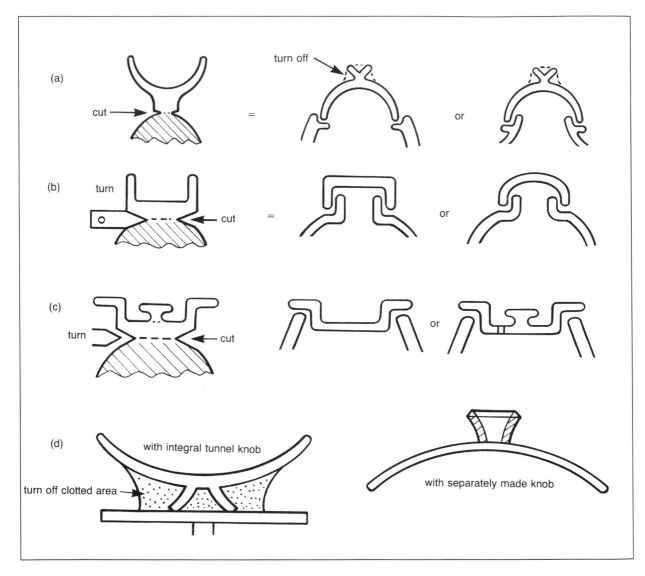

Fig 40 Some suggestions: (a) simple lid, thrown and cut off hump, knob turned; (b) without knob; (c) teapot or storage jar lids; (d) shallow bowl shape with integral turned knob or turned flat to receive a separately made knob later.

PROJECT – THROW A LIDDED BOWL

Step 1 Throw a cylindrical pot with an inward sloping neck; use a strangulation grip to restrict the neck.
Step 2 Close up completely, as shown overleaf, and/or further restrict using a rib, ruler or hand pressure.

Step 3 Remove and allow to stiffen to leather hard. Replace on a dry wheel-head, centre by tapping and secure with three plugs of clay.
Step 4 Allow the wheel to revolve slowly and cut gently through the wall of the pot to release the top section (do not push the needle straight through in one place; instead, carve through slowly).

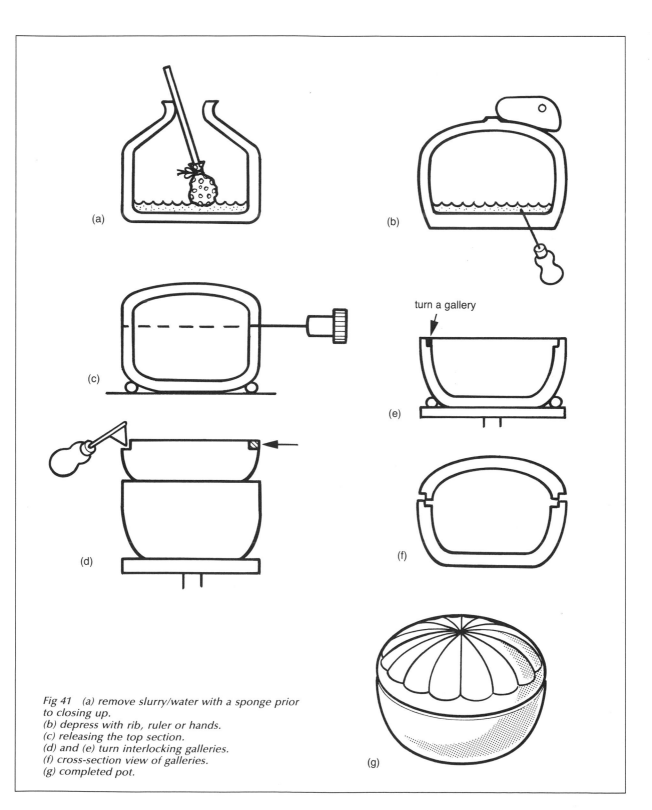

Fig 41 (a) remove slurry/water with a sponge prior to closing up.
(b) depress with rib, ruler or hands.
(c) releasing the top section.
(d) and (e) turn interlocking galleries.
(f) cross-section view of galleries.
(g) completed pot.

turn a gallery

Fig 42 Closing a neck: (a) 'strangulation' grip.

(b) closed up.

(c) consolidating the join using a rib.

(d) The finished pot, still on the wheel.

Step 5 Invert the lid section on to the base. Turn off the outer rim to form a gallery. Take off half the thickness. Remove the lid and put it aside.

Step 6 Turn the inner gallery on the base section, checking its fit by offering up the lid.

Step 7 Replace the lid, check for an even fit, and fettle or turn lightly across the join to effect a perfect match.

TIPS

- Don't make the fit too snug; it might not actually fit later.
- Allow the pieces to dry out slowly, and dry and biscuit-fire both bowl and lid together.
- Wherever possible, glaze-fire lids *in situ* to ensure mutual fit in spite of any movement in the firing.

Note The base may also require turning. If it has been thrown well and cut off carefully with a twisted wire, it may not need anything other than a perfunctory trim to clean up the foot. Functional or decorative handles, knobs or other appendages can be added while the piece is still leather hard. A simple, impressed decoration might be most suitable (*see* Chapter 6).

PROJECT – MAKE A TEAPOT

Having examined the design of this apparently complex ware in an earlier section (*see* Chapter 1), now consider the practical requirements. In reality, a teapot is a more or less cylindrical pot with the following additions: a spout (a), thrown off the hump as above, modelled or pinched; a lid (b), possibly thrown as a shallow bowl as above; and a handle (c) which could be pulled in the traditional way, rolled, cut or modelled, depending on the overall design. Alternatively, the handle might be made of cane and attached to lugs on the shoulder of the pot.

The Body

Step 1 Prepare a supply of clay. Weigh out two or three balls, each weighing 3–6lb (1.4–2.7kg).

Fig 43 Basic teapot shapes.

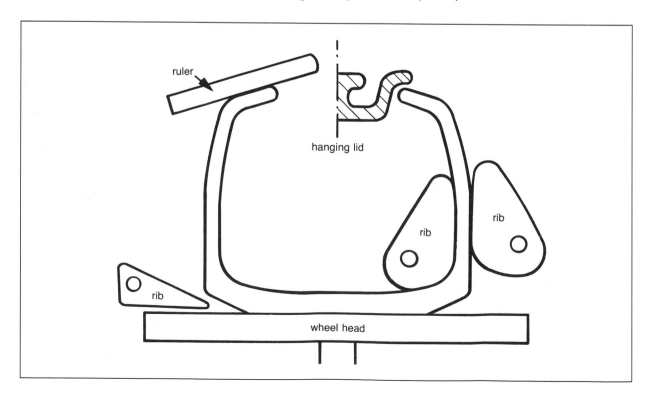

Throw these to form the bodies of the teapots. Keep the forms simple, and a little taller than you think is perhaps appropriate. Try to leave only enough thickness at the lower (foot) part to support the rest of the body. This should easily be removed before the pots are cut off, thereby reducing or eliminating the need for turning.

Step 2 Use a rib, ruler or modelling tool to narrow the shoulder. Aim to throw the rim so that it will take well to a hanging lid.

Step 3 Use ribs to shape and trim the profile, both inside and out as necessary.

Step 4 Release the pot using a very tight nylon-wire cutter and water, sliding it off on to a wet bat or board. Sponge away any water before leaving the pot to stiffen. You might also try throwing directly on to a wooden bat to prevent the risk of distortion when removing the body from the wheel. Additionally, the use of a twisted wire to cut the base, coupled with the application of a sheet of newspaper across the rim of the teapot body, will prevent distortion during removal.

The Lid

Step 1 Measure the first teapot lip with a calliper and endeavour to throw subsequent pots to the same size – the lids should then be interchangeable.

Step 2 Throw the lid off the hump or individually, whichever is found to be easiest. Make the initial shapes taller and more V-shaped than inclination might suggest.

Step 3 Make several spare lids so that the best looking and fitting can be selected for use with each pot.

Fig 45 (a and b)   Checking lid size for fit.

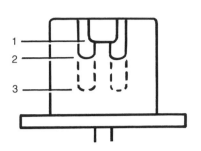

Fig 46 (a) open the clay to produce a central protuberance from which to form the knob.

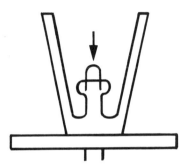

(b) gently depress centre. Use a rib or 6in ruler inside rim to broaden – see (iii).

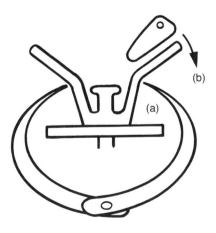

(c) do not over-flatten. A gentle transition from (a) to (b) will give tolerance to the fit. Measure with callipers to match sizes of rim and lid.

The Spout

You will probably prefer to throw the spout off the hump, as above. Aim to produce tall, narrow shapes similar to cooling towers, collared up and in by the strangulation method. Make at least three spouts per pot to allow for selection, and so that they can be cut and shaped to fit.

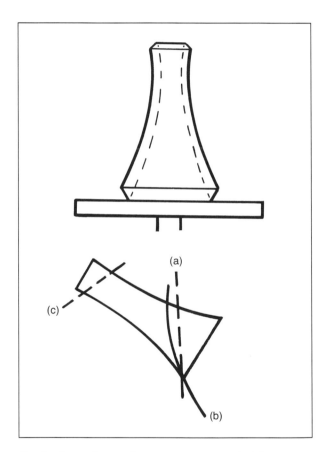

Fig 47 Cut and pare off excess spout material. Offer up to parent body as you trim to check for fit. (a) and/or (b) will require some care; (c) may not require cutting.

The Handle

While the thrown components are stiffening up to leather hard, a start can be made on the handles. The traditional pulling method will require both adequate spares to allow for wastage, and time to preform and stiffen prior to attachment. If cane handles are appropriate and available, only their

Fig 48   Rolling and shaping textured handles.

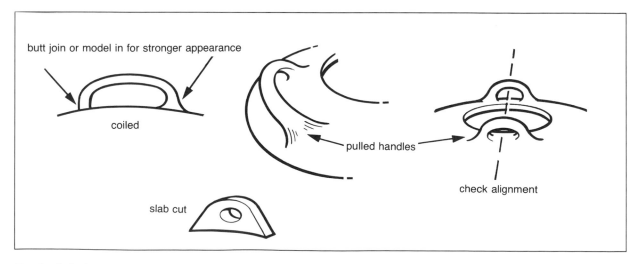

Fig 49   Coiled, pulled or slabbed lugs can be attached to receive cane handles.

Fig 50   Pulling a handle.

lugs will need to be made. The simplest lugs are crated from coils of appropriate length and thickness, these being attached to the shoulder of the parent pot.

It is important that both the handle and pot surfaces to be joined are of similar consistency and that both sides of the join are well scored and slipped. Maximum strength is required for any handle; small contact areas leave no room for weaknesses. Such joins can be vulnerable to tensions caused by uneven shrinkage during the drying-out process: long, slow drying is better than quick, uneven drying.

When the teapot is complete, allow it to dry out with the appropriate lid in place, either in a damp cupboard or inside a plastic bag. Slow, careful drying is essential for all complex forms; this advice applies to all the suggested projects and most of the pieces illustrated within this book. Similarly, the use of hot-air strippers or hair-driers to speed up any of the processes encountered calls for careful handling. Their use will undoubtedly enable quicker assembly, a convenience most potters welcome.

4

Hand-Building Techniques

Traditionally, there are three main hand-building methods: pinching, or making thumb pots; coiling; and slab-building. None of the methods requires much mention here except to reiterate the characteristics each can bring to the projects suggested later in this chapter.

THUMB POTS

Thumb or pinch pots are, as the name implies, simply worked with the fingers and thumbs to produce characteristically small, well-considered forms. The pots rely on touch almost as much as visual sensitivity for their often subtle shapes; the process encourages a unique awareness of the properties of clay, and as such has been used in the past to both introduce the material and to heighten awareness of form.

COIL POTS

Coiling is usually considered an excellent building process for the production of large, often strong, vigorous forms, these being often eccentric and sometimes sculptural. Growth is steady, affording control over the material and outcome, as well as opportunity to reflect on future development. The basic principle is that a form is built up from an appropriate base by stacking coils or rings of clay one on top of another, adjusting the diameter of the coils to increase or diminish the profile width, and modelling and/or joining the coils together, sometimes with slip.

SLAB POTS

Slabbing consists of cutting and assembling rolled-out or cut slabs into, usually, rectilinear constructions such as boxes. Slab-building could almost be seen as a cross between carpentry and dressmaking, in that patterns can be designed and used to prefabricate component parts prior to joining. The normal assumption is that the slabs will be flat, but a traditional contradiction to this is evident in the production of press-moulded dishes. Here, slabs are encouraged to conform to the preformed, usually female, contours of a simple one-piece mould. Preformed slabs therefore need not necessarily be restricted to a flat format, and by allowing rolled-out slabs to adapt to either female (concave) formers or to male (convex) supports, a wide variety of prefabricated components can be produced.

COMBINED BUILDING TECHNIQUES

There is nothing new about using a combination of techniques. Pinched appendages, such as spouts and ears, have often been attached to thrown or coiled wares. Similarly, both flat and curved or dished slabs have been incorporated into sculptural pieces, thereby enabling the maker to utilize the properties of several processes in the realization of complex forms.

The metaphorical escape from flat, slabbed rectilinear forms, and the addition of prefabricated hand-formed components can be illustrated by the following simple project.

PROJECT – TEAPOT OR COFFEE-POT

First, a simple 'box form' body can be constructed in slabs, this having a flat top, two sides and two ends, and a base/bottom. From this basic form, several variations are possible.

Further, subtle forms can be achieved by inducing a distortion of the flat surfaces – if one pair of side walls is cut with *slightly* curved edges, the

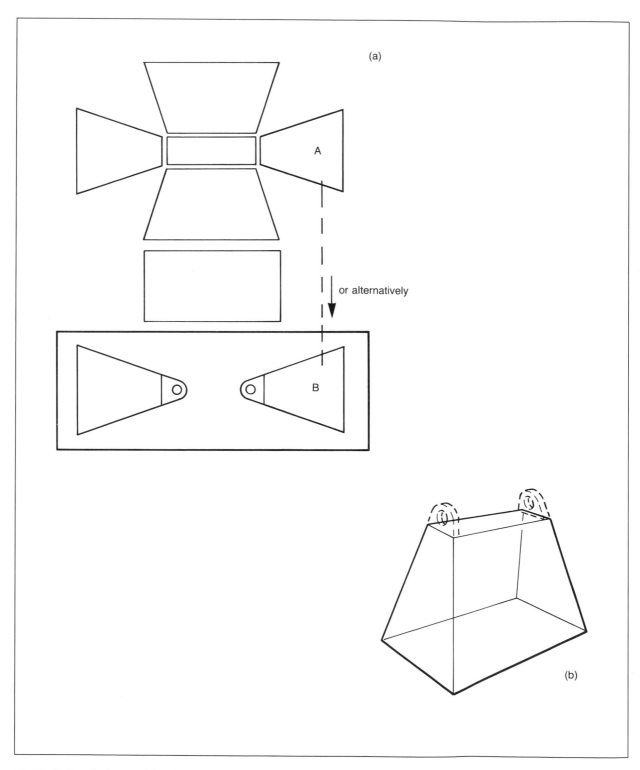

(a)

A

or alternatively

B

(b)

Fig 51   Pattern for teapot slabs; this can be altered and refined at the maquette stage (b).

Fig 52   Cut out to form lid. Spout: slabbed and pinched. Handle: preformed slab/strip, or pulled.

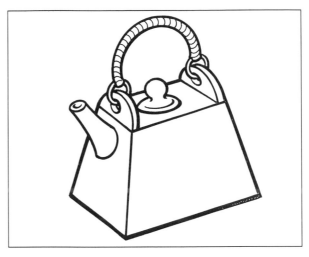

Fig 53   Cane handle attached to integral lugs on end slabs; spout thrown or pinched.

form will be distorted somewhat to accommodate the new dimensions and attendant stresses. All component parts could be given slightly curved edges, or you could restrict this to only the base and top, two sides, and so on.

Instead of using flat slabs for the sides (or cheeks) of the vessel, it is possible to preform convex slabs. These, while still in a soft, leather state, can be trimmed and coaxed into place to break away from the confines of a flat format and to afford more volume, both visually and practically.

Fig 54   Altering the proportions could produce a coffee pot. In simpler format it could be used as a jug.

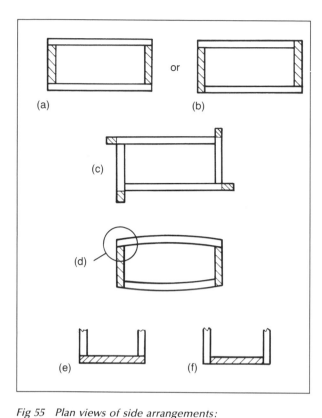

Fig 55 Plan views of side arrangements:
(a) and (b) simple butt joins.
(c) excess can be trimmed off and fettled after assembly.
(d) requires careful trimming.
(e) always build up from a base, not as in (f), and always build on a board.

Design

It is obviously possible to develop simple design ideas in two dimensions – for example, permutations and variations of overall dimensions can be explored to obtain an overview of proportion. Height to width, width to breadth and other proportions can be so examined. However, drawing up perspective views that incorporate curved edges as well as simple dimensions demands prediction and is likely to be difficult, if not impossible.

To discover three-dimensional outcomes it is more informative to actually work in 3D. Trial and error, using actual slabs of clay, is perhaps one way forward, but making use of cardboard cut-outs, adhesive tape and scissors or a craft knife is more likely to be quicker. By constructing maquettes (3D sketches) in this way, difficulties and possibilities can be highlighted in much less time than it takes to prepare slabs. A maquette can later be modified with comparative ease, deconstructed and then used as a pattern. To state the obvious, remember that the eventual use of clay slabs will involve thicknesses not encountered with card, so joins, overlaps, bases and the like will have to be taken into account. Be prepared for any necessary fine tuning at the assembly stage.

Construction

Having designed a vessel and produced patterns

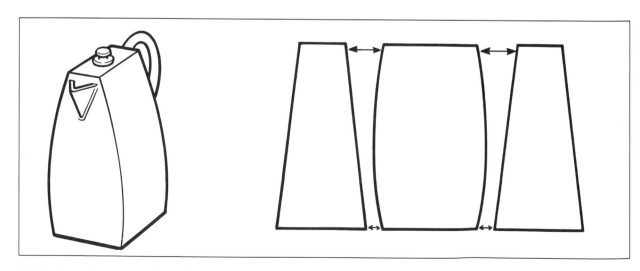

Fig 56 Excessive curves will cause distortions.

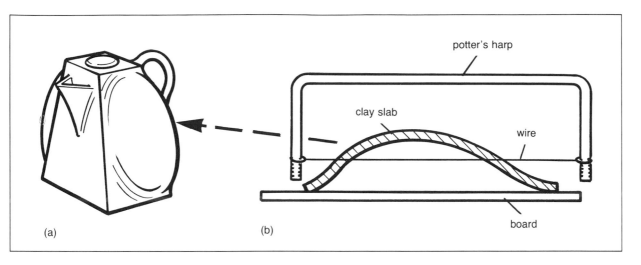

Fig 57 (a) convex slabs utilized to form sides of pot. (b) a preformed slab, just stiff enough to maintain shape, can be trimmed with a potter's harp.

from maquettes, there will be a need to take into account means of joining that incorporate curves and varying degrees of thickness. Remember here that ceramics is not a precise art and that the raw

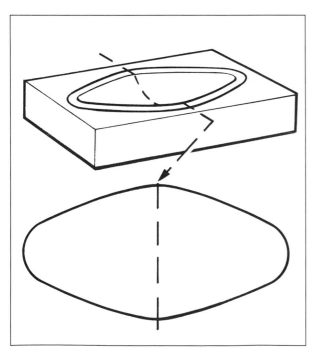

Fig 58 Press-moulded dish could provide two side sections.

material is malleable – it can, to some extent at least, be trimmed, bent and moulded into conformity. Patient trimming and persuasion is therefore required, together with an awareness of the nature of the material you are using – in other words, the condition or plasticity of the prefabricated components.

If a suitable plaster mould is available, you can use it to make a symmetrical pair of sides. The basic body can be designed and constructed without too much difficulty. A simple bell shape made from a pressed dish by cutting and joining can then be stuck down firmly on to an untrimmed slab so that an exact fit will be obtained. Joints should be given careful attention. Score all surfaces that are to be joined, and 'glue' them with slip made from the same clay body as that of the slabs. Wherever possible, model in the join, adding a thin coil of clay to it, particularly on the inside surface.

Careful planning is necessary to ensure access to the major joins. If the base slab is added last, as above, other joins can be strengthened on the inside before the form is closed up. The base can be secured mainly from the outside, but access will be afforded through the lid aperture. Use a modelling tool or long-handled paintbrush to clean, slip and smooth the final base join.

It is also important to ensure that all the component parts are of the same leather-hard consistency, and that none is left to get too hard before joining.

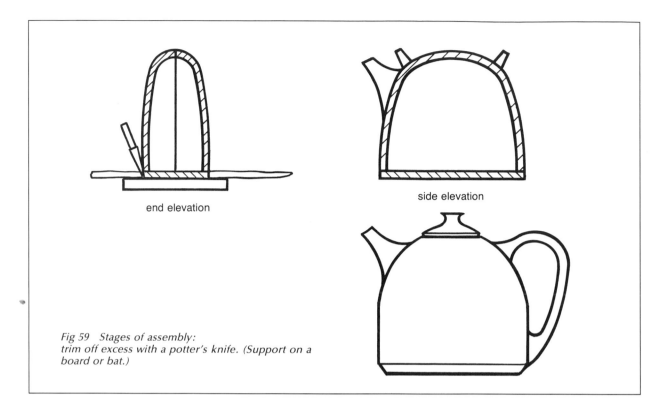

end elevation

side elevation

*Fig 59 Stages of assembly:
trim off excess with a potter's knife. (Support on a
board or bat.)*

The individual parts will require careful storing and protection against premature drying, and this will also be true for additional details such as the handle, spout, lid and/or lugs. Therefore, when the main body is fully assembled, ensure that it is wrapped up well in an airtight plastic bag to prevent further hardening.

General Advice

In any situation where joins are required between component parts, the clay needs to be of a uniform, leather-hard consistency. Where one part is allowed to dry out more than another, some shrinkage will have already taken place and stress will result at the join when the second part starts to shrink. The shrinkage rate should ideally be even throughout. Major problem areas can be handles, which are likely to be softer than the body when joined and tend to dry out more quickly if exposed to a drying atmosphere.

Regardless of production methods, it is necessary to bring all components to the same state of leather, or cheese hardness prior to assembly. It is also advisable to slow down final drying by bagging the complete piece. This enables consolidation of all parts so that any differences in wet/dry consistencies can, to a certain extent, be evened out. Bagging will also prevent premature drying out of thin appendages and reduce the risk of such parts pulling off as they dry and shrink.

The above advice is true for all building combinations – slabbed, coiled, thrown, cast or extruded components. Careful planning will help to avoid or prevent accidents and problems which might otherwise appear during drying or firing.

PROJECT – GARDEN PLANTER

Concept

The various skills, techniques and processes involved in ceramics are interrelated and interdependent, and are best seen as a means rather than an end; the brilliant thrower who cannot make handles cannot make a mug. The following project assumes that processes and techniques can be combined deliberately in order to free the potter from convention, leading eventually to innovation and a challenging new awareness of exploration.

The project tends to make use of traditional craft approaches while at the same time apparently rejecting them. The idea is twofold: to make a utilitarian piece which fulfils its intended purpose; and to allow the piece to grow in a process-led and material-led way, so that the building is spontaneous according to instinct, imagination and responding perhaps to the dictates of the material.

DESIGN

In very general terms it helps to have some idea of what is actually envisaged – some overall dimensions and a roughly conceived shape should be sufficient.

The eventual planter will be oval in plan (more or less). The pot will be fairly large, will probably be wider than it is high, and it may widen slightly as it grows up from its base. In terms of visual appearance, the above description is probably all that is necessary by way of design.

Before suggesting the means of building the piece, however, it is necessary to examine one or two other factors affecting its design:

• It is to be built using crude hand-building techniques. A grogged body will assist building, having less shrinkage than a very fine body. The grog will afford some support to the structure. Any raku clay or crank material is appropriate.
• The vessel is to be used outdoors. Outdoor pieces are often subjected to frost, and a porous body is more likely to be affected by this. It will be appropriate, therefore, to vitrify the ware by firing up to stoneware temperature, rendering the body virtually non-porous. Traditional terracotta garden pots have a characteristically warm, pleasant appearance, but they do require protection against freezing. Stoneware should prove much less prone to damage.
• The piece will not be glazed. Rather than glazing the planter, which will, in practical terms, be relatively non-absorbent, it can be decorated by the application of oxides. Red iron oxide and/or manganese dioxide will stain the surfaces in natural, mineral tones which are unlikely to give offence.

Building

First, ensure that there is a board available upon which the piece can be built. To an extent, this board will determine the size of the planter and will facilitate moving, covering and storing during the building process.

Base

Step 1   Flatten a 5–10lb (2.3–4.5kg) lump of clay into an oval slab. Initially, thump or press it down, then finish by rolling it on to a sheet of canvas. The thickness of the slab will depend on its size, but should be ¼–½in (0.75–1.5cm) thick.

Step 2   With care and a little luck, a reasonably even oval outline can be achieved. If necessary, or desired, a precise shape can be drawn on and trimmed out at this stage, working on the base board. Three or four drainage holes could also be cut through the base if required.

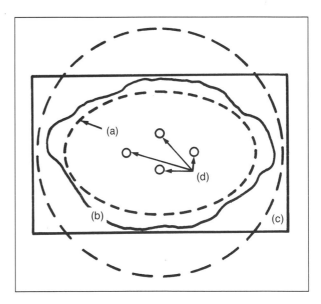

Fig 60   Roughly oval slab supported on bat or board (c).
(a) neatly trimmed base shape or,
(b) free-formed, arbitrary, base.
(d) drainage holes.

Step 3   If the base can be supported on a bench whirler or banding wheel the work can be turned easily without any need to actually handle the pot. It also allows the piece to be seen quickly from

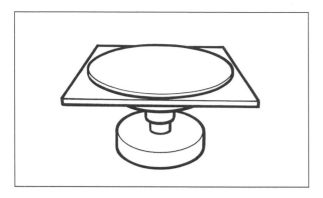

Fig 61   Centralize board and slab on a banding wheel.

any angle, thereby enabling checks to be made on profile shape and unity of texture and pattern development.

Walls

Step 1   To obtain a positive foundation, apply one coil in the traditional manner – hand-roll the coil to a similar thickness to the base, then score the base and apply slip. Place the coil carefully *in situ* and model it gently but firmly inside and out into place on the slab. This base will be both physically solid and have visual strength.

Step 2   On to this low wall can now be built slabs chunks, or pressed pieces of clay. Smallish lumps of clay can be rolled out roughly, possibly on to textured surfaces, to form arbitrarily shaped pieces (these can be rolled out in reasonable quantity and allowed to stiffen a little prior to attachment). Similarly, slices of clay can be cut from rough lumps that have interesting surface qualities. Thicker areas can be reduced by carving away from the inside, using a looped modelling tool.

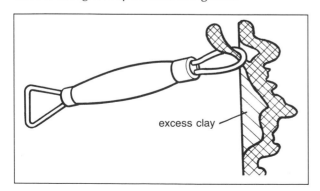

excess clay

Fig 62.

The process of constructing the walls is a little bit like dry-stone walling: pieces are selected to fit (more or less) and to create an arbitrary pattern within the overall structure. Holes and cracks that remain can be both decorative and practical, providing drainage and even openings through which plants may trail and grow. At points of contact, however, it is essential to achieve strong joins. Use scoring, slip and firm modelling to weld up the inside so that the casual chaos outside is not achieved at the cost of weakness and eventual collapse.

The first such piece I made was an attempt to create an impression of something that had been blown together; unfortunately, it turned out to be just that as it survived the drying process but fell to pieces during the biscuit-fire. Therefore, more, not less attention to technique is required where weaknesses are built into a structure. Ordeal by fire is pretty much what occurs – any structural inadequacy will be sought out, tested and judged in the kiln! Particular attention must therefore be paid to all joins and weaknesses.

Fig 63   Garden planter.

Fig 64 Garden planter.

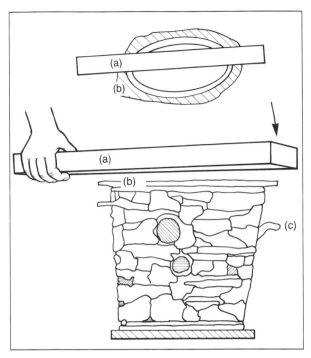

Fig 66 Levelling the top. Tap down the top making contact with the 'bat' on both sides simultaneously – turn (on the banding wheel) while beating down.
(a) use a suitable piece of timber to consolidate the rim. (b) a thick coil could be used to form a strong lip or rim. (c) chunky appendages can serve as handles.

Rim

When the piece nears its desired height, it is necessary to level off the building chunks, first by size and then by tapping. The finished lip or rim can then be built on with slabs or a thick coil that is beaten down.

Feet

These can be added to assist drainage and to improve the overall appearance of the piece. Some light appearing under the base will help to lessen the lumpen, earthbound appearance of any wide, flat base and will work better than pebbles shoved underneath. You can either try to integrate the feet with the overall appearance of the planter, or you could try something entirely contrasting. On one pot, lions' feet might actually seem right, while on another, lumps that are similar to those used elsewhere in the structure may be better. Whatever the style, use three feet as they will always provide

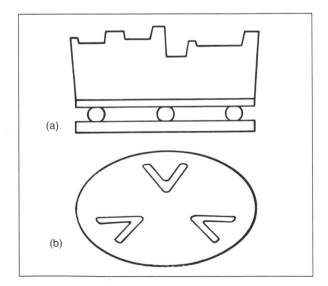

Fig 65 (a) three balls of clay compressed by the planter to form simple disc-shaped feet.
(b) three folded slabs allowed to flatten a little.

a stable base. Position the feet to afford best balance.

If the planter can be built quickly enough to ensure that it is leather hard throughout, and can therefore be inverted safely, attach the feet on completion. Alternatively, the feet can be added at some point during construction by lifting the vessel and lowering it on to pre-located feet. That is to say, put the feet in position on a base board ready to receive the pot as it is placed on top of them. With scoring and slip, the weight of the part-built pot will ensure a good join.

Decorating and Firing

Both of these topics will be dealt with in greater depth elsewhere (see Chapters 6 and 9), but simple solutions only are required in this instance.

Step 1 After careful, total drying, the planter should be biscuit-fired to enable safe handling.

Step 2 When cool, sponge on a wash of manganese dioxide liberally, allowing it to run down into depressions and joins where it will deposit a thickish coat of pigment. Carefully wipe off oxide from raised surfaces with a clean sponge. The resulting dark deposits in crevasses and lighter high spots will emphasize contrasts, textures and patterns. A subsequent stoneware firing will fuse the oxide and vitrify the clay; glazing is not necessary.

Step 3 Pots with feet should be fired upside-down to prevent sagging in the fire at high stoneware temperatures. Several pots without feet could be fired (where kiln size permits) one on top of another, head to tail, and stacked as in a biscuit-firing.

Once-Firing

There is no reason why such pieces should not be once-fired; if unfired raw clay is subjected to the decoration process suggested above, there could well be problems:

- Handling a large, unfired piece would obviously increase chances of accidental damage.
- Sponging with washes might affect joins, putting the piece at risk, and would certainly create a surface very different from the one envisaged.
- Colour results might be muddy or smudged.
- Surface colour would wash off in an entirely

different way and would demand an extremely careful approach.

Pros and Cons

The greatest advantage in once-firing is obviously the saving of fuel. It also cuts down on handling time, and renders the piece safe and finished in one operation. The greatest, yet perhaps the only disadvantage is that at no time is the piece strong enough before firing to be handled, decorated or glazed (where necessary) without extreme care. I would generally err on the side of caution, particularly when handling other people's work.

PROJECT – COMBINED TECHNIQUE SCULPTURE

The completed piece made by the author (opposite) was built in the same way as the planter, with minor differences in design detail. The sculpture has no flat, slab base. It includes preformed, pinched parts, as well as rolled and flattened coils, rough-cut slabs and pieces cut from blocks of bagged clay. The latter, as with the planter, required some reduction in overall thickness in order to fit comfortably with other components. Excessive thickness was removed using a looped modelling tool working from behind – in other words, the inside – prior to attachment.

A well-grogged raku clay was used both for its open texture and low shrinkage characteristics. The piece was biscuit-fired for ease of handling, and was then washed with manganese dioxide as suggested for the planter. It was subsequently fired up to 1,265°C in an oxidized stoneware glaze firing.

This method of building can be used for utilitarian structures or for non-functional, sculptural pieces. It can be an enjoyable means of exploiting the natural properties of the material, making use of accidental, arbitrary texture and shape in the production of apparently casual, spontaneous pieces. It can also be channelled into the realization of sophisticated works that reflect conceptualization and control of the material in a unique sculptural way. That is to say that sculpture, like painting, is usually capable of being changed or modified; such work can be allowed to develop and evolve throughout the realization process.

Fig 67 (a) sculptural form.

(b) sculptural form: building in T-material.

With a painting, the starting point will have been lost or disguised beneath later developments, but this is not the case with a ceramic piece. If the piece starts from an oval base, it is most probable that it will finish with it, and beyond an almost indefinable point in the development of the piece it will be impossible to change what went before as clay becomes less malleable during the process of drying, restricting and eventually excluding modification. In this respect, at least, it is important to recognize that preconceived ideas of the piece can be a help rather than a hindrance.

Building the Piece

The Soggy Bottom Syndrome

A well-considered start to the piece will literally and aesthetically support later development of the form, where a weak foundation would not. You may well have seen examples of coiled pots which epitomize the latter. A person's first attempt at a coiled pot develops until the upper portion is well made, formed and finished. However, the inescapable, shaky foundation completely detracts from eventual accomplishment, highlighting a lack of conceptual strength and initial competence.

Tips on Building

One of the main objectives when building a piece is to gain height. Coil-building is less quick than using slabs, although the character of the result is likely to be different. That said, slabs that are not stiff enough to support their own weight will inevitably slump – it is useful to roll out a range of sizes and shapes, allowing them to stiffen before incorporating them into the structure.

Step 1 Lay out the slabs on an absorbent surface such as a piece of timber or, preferably, plaster slabs.

Step 2 If the stiffening time seems too long, causing unnecessary delay, use a hair-drier or electric paint-stripper to force the pieces to dry. Take care not to overdry the pieces; cheese hard is about right.

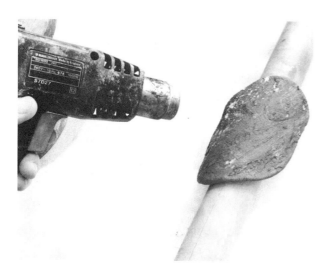

Fig 68 Force drying using an electric paint-stripper.

Step 3 When the slabs are almost stiff enough, lay them out on a plastic sheet to prevent further drying, and cover them with another sheet. In this way you have control over the condition of each piece.

Step 4 Conversely, if the pieces are found to have stiffened too much, they may soften sufficiently if laid out on damp cloth, covered with more damp cloth and plastic, and then left to absorb a little moisture.

Potters have been known to soften appendages (spouts, handles and so on) by immersing them briefly in water, but the 'sweating' process described in Step 4 above seems safer and more likely to succeed, and is considered better practice. It would be better, in any event, to avoid excessive stiffening, and hence delay and uncertainty, wherever possible.

Coils Roll out a coil about twice normal thickness – at least twice the thickness of the base. Lay the coil on a dry, absorbent surface and flatten it carefully using a rolling pin, or pat it down with a piece of wood. Roll it on to a rough surface to pick up texture – sawn, unplaned planks could be used, or anything else with an interesting surface, such as coarse material, nylon mesh or rubber matting. The impressed surface pattern or texture will then be presented as the outside of the flattened section, and built into place as and where it seems appropriate. Such flattened coils can be bent to fit against other pieces, or left straight.

Fig 69 Carefully flattening a thick coil.

Slabs These can also be rolled out on a textured surface, trimmed as necessary and then pieced together with coils and/or other odd-shaped pieces to form the wall of the sculpture.

Balls These can be made to fill unwanted gaps in the walls. Make a clay ball which will just about pass through the hole. Place it in the gap, then squeeze it gently from both sides at once so that it flattens into a disc, expands to fit the hole exactly, and hence introduces a new element to the outside pattern.

Unity of Design A device similar to a flattened ball can be used as an erratic repeat, helping to achieve a sense of overall unity in the pattern.

Long, conventional coils will create lines linking disparate elements, sometimes pulling them together; a complete coil or strip placed along the top and bottom will give a finished look to the whole.

Materials

Large, chunky pieces requiring a robust, not to say crude, visual appearance, can be constructed from heavily grogged bodies. If finer, more sophisticated forms are required, then it may be worth using a specialist body such as T-material. This is an exceptionally high-quality clay, having a white, coarse body with amazing wet strength. It has a wide firing range, good glaze acceptance and is superb for raku, where its whiteness gives excellent colour response and strength is afforded through its grog content. Although it is nearly three times the price of raku bodies, T-material can still be economically viable due to its strength – it enables work to be made thinner and lighter, thereby allowing a bag of raw material to go further.

TIPS

If an appendage breaks away totally it may be possible to replace it safely using vinegar. Small chips can be stuck back on in this manner. Apply vinegar to the surfaces to be joined using a small brush (sometimes fine scoring is useful). Hold the pieces together under firm, gentle pressure if possible. This method usually works with green, dry ware *prior* to biscuit-firing.

Summary

Sculptural forms can be both interesting and challenging to produce. The potter's imagination can be allowed full rein, perhaps following suggested patterns of landscape, geology and the like, while at the same time following a growing form which is not tied to conventional pot forms or surface decoration.

5

Assemblage

There have always been craftspeople who are capable of throwing or coiling large pots, but many such pieces have been, and still are, produced by assembling several smaller, prefabricated sections. Often, a mix of different processes is used to achieve a complete artefact.

In this chapter I indicate some such combinations and give examples of their use, but without suggesting a definitive list or implying that combinations not mentioned cannot be considered. The main aim in this is to suggest possibilities and give a little support. It is hoped from this that the reader may develop his or her own avenues of exploration, thereby leading to an own-brand development of creative expression. The intention is definitely not to dictate *only ways* of doing *only things*, if such phraseology can be followed. Projects should be seen as starting points from which to follow your own inclinations, and to utilize your initiative and imagination.

Assumptions are often made that the art or craft of throwing requires each piece to be achieved in one effort. To throw a large vase, for example, requires control over a large lump of clay, this involving great strength. Another assumption seems to be that only complete forms should be made, regardless of size. However, if you can only manage 3–4lb (1.4–1.8kg) lumps, why not pre-design an 8–10lb (3.6–4.5kg) vase which is constructed in two or three sections.

PLAY YOUR WAY IN

Preconceived ideas of assemblage can be inhibiting and frustrating. A fun way to overcome this is as follows:

Step 1   Prepare a quantity of clay sufficient for a couple of hours throwing – six to twelve balls of clay each weighing approximately 2lb (0.9kg).

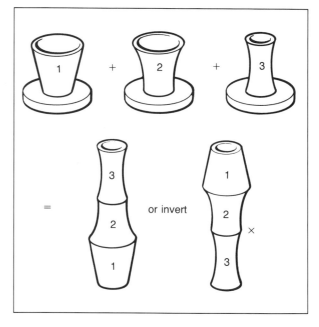

Fig 70   *Allow sections to stiffen; turn, score and slip; assemble.*

Step 2   Cover all but the first ball with plastic to prevent premature stiffening. Have a supply of boards ready to receive pots, and ensure that you have the necessary tools (a natural sponge; a small, wooden dog-ear tool, modelling tool or turning tool; and potter's wire for cutting off).

Step 3   Proceed by throwing virtually any shape that takes your fancy. Finish it off as for a serious pot – in other words, clean and trim it, and carefully remove it from wheel-head. Then throw the next pot, and the next, until you have used up all the balls of clay. Some attempts may come to nothing, but on the other hand several, or many, will be successful.

Step 4   You should have a range of assorted, possibly rather crude pots which require stiffening and turning. When leather hard, and before turning,

Fig 71   Throwing sections: (a) checking diameter with callipers.

(b) turning and scoring.

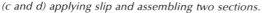

(c and d) applying slip and assembling two sections.

try matching up two or more pieces. Attempt to gain height by piling sections on top of each other, at the same time building a visually interesting structure. Find the best fits and decide on order of assembly. Where necessary, turn off excess clay and turn out unwanted bottoms. Score all surfaces to be joined, slip and assemble. Be careful not to allow the sections to stiffen too much or too unevenly. Clean up and disguise all joins, inside and out, by turning or fettling with a potter's steel kidney.

Step 5 If you find that none of the pieces actually fit together then make some more, bearing in mind the eventual purpose of the pieces. At the same time, wrap up the first batch carefully, saving them in case they match subsequent offerings.

DECONSTRUCTION/RECONSTRUCTION

Someone once said that it is necessary to destroy in order to create. Try cutting and reassembling some thrown shapes to see what you can achieve. Start with a simple cylinder, cutting across the sec-

tion at several points and at different angles; this may suggest variations which may be worthy of development. Alternatively, cut the cylinder vertically and reassemble it.

PROJECT – THROWN, CUT AND REASSEMBLED DISH

Step 1 Throw a shallow dish, say 12–14in (30–35cm) in diameter and 2–4in (5–10cm) deep. For ease of removal, throw on a bat. There are two options here: throw the piece with no bottom, and use a rib or modelling tool to trim the foot inside and out (option A); or allow for the removal of the base when leather hard (option B). Release the piece from the bat by cutting with a nylon wire. You can use a home-made rib, cut from credit card, to form a suitable rim.

Step 2 Roll out a slab of clay which is nearly the same thickness as the thrown wall sections. It should be large enough for the thrown section to sit upon, with some spare for trimming.

Step 3 Allow both pieces to stiffen to leather

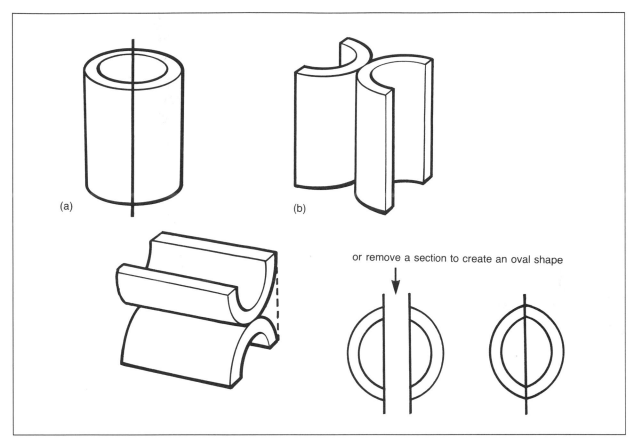

Fig 72   Vertical cuts.

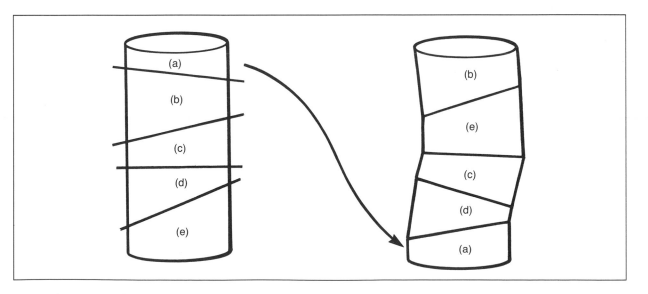

Fig 73   Reconstructed cylinder.

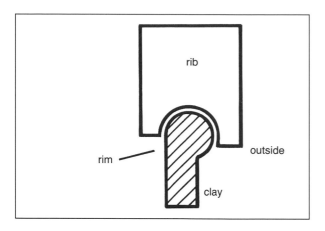

Fig 74   Forming a rim using a home-made rib.

hard. Take care not to allow the rolled slab to dry out too much; if necessary, cover the rolled slab with a sheet of plastic to allow the thrown part extra time.

Step 4   Option B – turn out the foot/base to achieve an open form.

Step 5   Options A and B – carefully measure and mark a middle section for removal. In other words, cut out sections of wall to reduce the circle to an oval plan. Score and slip the sections carefully, then bring them together to re-form the sides/ walls of the vessel.

Step 6   Invert the piece, using bats to support the open form if necessary. Score and slip the walls and base. It is usually possible to handle the wall

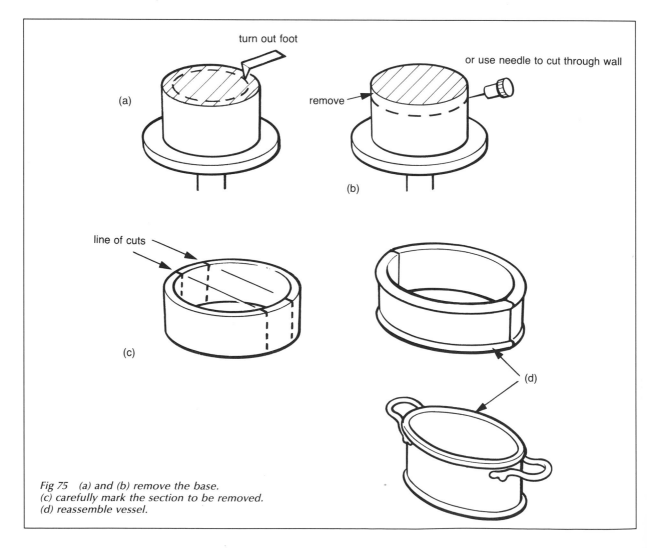

Fig 75   (a) and (b) remove the base.
(c) carefully mark the section to be removed.
(d) reassemble vessel.

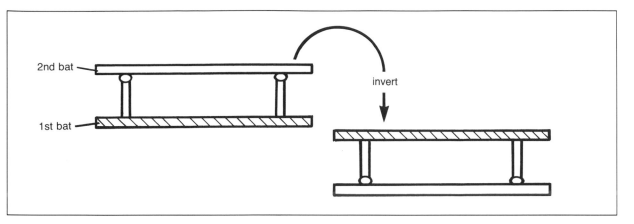

Fig 76   Invert a pot using two bats.

section safely at this stage as it should be well stiffened, thus it is possible to offer up the wall to its base to mark the location of scoring and slip.

Step 7   After slipping, lower the wall section into place on the base, applying firm but gentle pressure to squeeze out excess slip. The inside join should then be smoothed in to consolidate the join and to obtain a pleasing, rounded section at the foot. Ensure the slab is supported on a bat or board.

Step 8   The slab should then be trimmed, allowing a rim of approximately ¼in (0.6cm) on the outside of the foot. Place the bat supporting the dish on to a bench whirler, and use another flexible friend to form a ribbed foot-ring by carefully working around as you revolve the dish slowly.

Fig 77   Gratin dish by Judith Wensley.

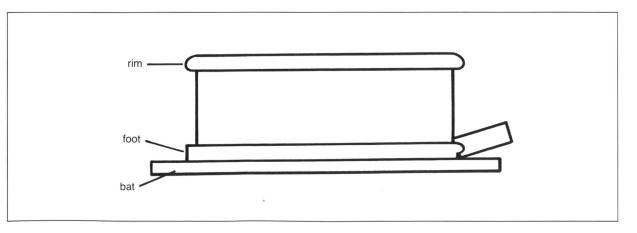

Fig 78   Finishing the foot.

Fig 79   An assortment of 'ribs'.

Ribs can range in size and shape (as shown above), as well as intended use, according to individual needs. If you have use for a rib you will almost certainly have to develop and make your own, probably by trial and error. The advantage of this is, of course, that your own ribs impart a unique stamp on your work while, hopefully, giving it a unified, professional look.

PROJECT – THROWN AND SLABBED VESSEL

The following project is based on a modicum of philosophy: if the piece has an appropriate beginning and end (top and bottom), the middle will probably take care of itself. Basically, the idea is to use thrown sections for the top and bottom, and slabs (and possibly some coils to assist at the transitional stages) for the middle section. Given that

the relationship between the two extremities is right, almost anything can be done to the body section without risk of a major aesthetic disaster.

Step 1   Throw a series of varied cooling tower shapes, but with broader, more generous feet/bases, and with stronger, more positive lips. Remember that it is the lip here that counts, and how it will eventually work with a base. The lips of these sections can therefore be very overstated and robust or downright quirky, because they have nothing else with which to relate.

Step 2   Throw a similar number of bases. These could have the character of sturdy storage containers. If it is possible to identify a link between one of the tops and one of the bottoms, then so much the better. This returns us to the concepts of design mentioned in Chapter 4, suggesting some prior planning in the form of sketches or maquettes.

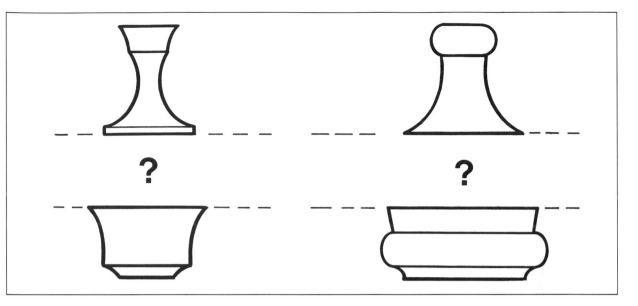

Fig 80   If the relationship between the top and bottom is harmonious, you can afford to be adventurous with the middle.

Alternatively, use the trial and error process, more spontaneously intuition-led than the former and hence perhaps more fun to go with. One piece may be larger or greater in diameter than the other, but provided you are happy with the relationship and can see the potential marrying of the two as an interesting idea then this is fine.

Step 3   Now try to fill in the gaps. Roll out slabs of clay which can then be preformed, trimmed and allowed to stiffen to leather hardness to match the consistency of the other pieces. Use a mould or lay the slab along a large cylinder such as a plastic or cardboard tube.

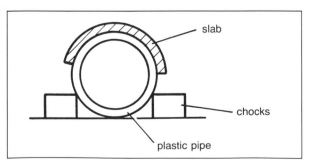

Fig. 81   Cross-section of slab on a cylindrical support to stiffen.

Step 4   Use coils, together with judicious carving of prefabricated parts, to achieve a comfortable transition from one form to another.

Step 5   Various appendages, lids, handles and modelled figures, either useful or absolutely nonsensical, can be added to create the final piece.

There has been a deliberate withholding of design suggestions for the above project in the hope that the reader's imagination will forge ahead unchecked.

MOULDS

Any male or female hump, lump, dent or depression can be used as a support for stiffening slabs, providing only that the same slab, once preformed, can be removed safely for use later on. Conventional plaster of Paris moulds release their charges easily due to their porosity, this minimizing the clay's tendency to stick to the surface. Similarly, wood or hardboard formers can be used. Fabrics such as canvas, sacking or sheeting will also enable retrieval of the slab, but polythene, plastic or any other non-porous surface is not suitable. Where it is necessary to use a support which is obviously going to cause trouble, careful preparation of its surface may solve the problem. Dust the surface first with talc or any powdered clay; sand will be picked up on the slab's surface, but this may be considered an added bonus rather than a problem.

Subtle preformed shapes can be obtained by using bent card or hardboard. Exaggerated forms can be achieved by using hammock-like slings in which to hang slabs. Alternatively, flop the slab over something – a heap of damp sand (possibly covered with a piece of material to avoid pick-up) can be moulded prior to being used as a male hump mould. Just use your imagination to explore the potential of this fun side of ceramics.

EXTRUSIONS

This technique has been borrowed from industrial processes such as the production of drainpipes, bricks and the like, and basically refers to what emerges from the rear end of a pug-mill. Normally solid, cylindrical slugs of clay emerge in plastic form, ready for storage or use. Modified barrels can produce extruded slugs with square or rectangular cross-sections; these can then be cut into lengths and used as bricks.

Some pug-mills and most extruders can be fitted with dies which make possible the production of solid round, hexagonal and square extrusions. In addition, some die sets include adaptors for making hollow-section tubes. It is possible for the handy DIY person to cut dies to fit a particular pug-mill or extruder using mild steel, hardwood or even perspex (I have even drilled and filed such dies to extrude handle strips). DIY dies for hollow extrusion are, however, rather more complicated.

Fig 82   (a) extruder dies.

The method for both the pugs I use is rugged and reasonably convenient. My small, hand-cranked, horizontal pug has a bolt-on expansion box to allow wider section dies to be used. You will get a lot of enjoyment and satisfaction out of playing with the various possibilities that become apparent as you utilize the various dies, and either combine extrusions together or with thrown or slabbed sections. I am not convinced that using extruders to produce coils is either necessary or makes the best use of the contraption's potential. On the other hand, assembling with the use of extrusions to achieve something otherwise very difficult does seem perfectly reasonable.

MODIFICATIONS

Clay's amazing plastic property allows it to be man-

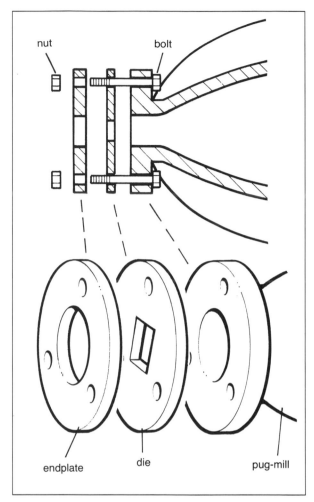

Fig 83   Pug-mill with extrusion die inserted; bolt together firmly.

(b) extrusions.

ipulated readily into almost any conceivable shape, and then stay that way. Consequently, forms as made can easily be modified. An obvious example exists in jugs: the spout is pulled, pinched and then dented into shape, sometimes with a little carefully applied force. Fat-bellied pot forms can be paddled when leather hard – patting with a flat, table-tennis-like bat to produce gently flattened vertical surfaces around the body. Thrown and slabbed pots can be rearranged by a similar application of force, ranging from tapping to bashing and even dropping from a height.

These processes sit uneasily somewhere between manufacture and decoration, particularly where the modification is a consideration of form

Fig 84   Modified jugs by Judith Wensley.

Fig 85   'Paddling'.

rather than function. To some extent this reflects the timing of the actions which depend on the condition of the clay for their precise outcomes. A thrown pot, for example, will accept some modifications immediately after its production, but attempts to alter it too much at that stage may soon result in its slumping beyond the intended point.

6

Decoration

Decoration of clay vessels is evident when viewing even the most primitive of ceramic forms. One might speculate that decoration began as a means of differentiation between domestic and ritual or ceremonial wares, or that potters might have chosen to mark their wares with symbols identifiable to themselves. For whatever reason, if one exists at all, the decoration of clay surfaces has become fairly standard practice in contemporary ceramics.

Obviously, many more methods, techniques and materials are available to contemporary potters than to potters in the distant past. The making and firing of wares has become more reliable, and decoration has developed alongside these advances. Certainly, the spectrum of ceramic colours alone has increased the possibilities open to both amateur and professional alike.

This is all great, but it is important that we do not lose sight of ceramic form. An important point to make here is that careful consideration must be made to ensure that the decoration and form compliment one another – an ornate form that is overly dressed may look inappropriate at best and downright silly at worst. Sometimes it is best to let the form stand for itself, with perhaps just a simple glaze.

If, on the other hand, you wish to have a free hand when it comes to the decorated surface, simple forms with clean lines and strong rims might provide a more satisfying and aesthetic solution. It has been argued for some time that there have been good pots and great decoration, but that the two rarely occur together. This view may be overstated, but an awareness of the argument may go some way towards resolving ill-conceived, overworked and ugly pots.

Having said all that, it would be useful to have both a shape and appropriate surface treatment in mind when you begin working on a pot. So many people make the mistake of building up a form without first giving consideration to shape, size, scale or proportion. Simple sketching is very useful because it gives you a chance to investigate all the possibilities for shape and also because it tests your ability to make what you have designed (*see* Chapter 1).

If you also consider decoration at the start of the building process, you will not eliminate many decorative techniques which, by waiting until the pot is fired, will be unavailable to you – for example, slip decoration or sgraffito, both done at the leather-hard stage. Decoration does not have to be a compromise if it is considered at the beginning, and not as an afterthought. Decorative techniques can be tried and experimented with before you commit your pot to an irretrievable process. Techniques such as brush or stencil work may be tried out on sheets of newspaper, and test tiles or thumb pots also offer another quick method of trying out many of the techniques available to you. Experimentation, coupled with careful recording, will help you to build up a library of techniques which can be drawn upon in any given situation.

Decorative processes must necessarily be ceramic; they must be capable of surviving some sort of firing process both to integrate with the ware and to endure. They seem, therefore, to fall into two distinct categories: 'in' and 'on'. The 'in' process refers to marks made in the clay itself or modelled on to it, and the 'on' process applies to colour.

'IN' DECORATION

Within the 'in' category can be included surface patterns or textures that reflect the nature of the building process (throwing marks) and the material (coarse or smooth clay). An extensively quoted example of this is the basket-weave texture, thought to have originated accidentally. The basket, a very early craft form, had its drawbacks as a container

Fig 86   Vigorous throwing marks.

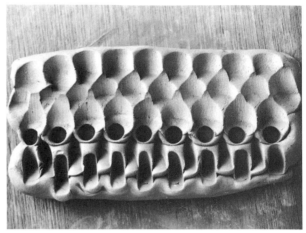

Fig 87   Pattern created by modelling using fingers or tools.

for small objects such as grain. In an attempt to overcome its shortcomings, clay was used to line the basket. When the basket perished it was placed on the fire as fuel. It has been suggested that this may have been an early discovery of pottery, as the clay would have baked in the fire. As pottery became more developed, the basket weave pattern remained as a decorative reminder of the past. Applied decorative detail such as relief modelling, non-functional spouts, handles and sprigging also fall into this category. Remember that robustly built and structured pieces will require perhaps no more than a simple glaze to render them suitable for their intended function, while at the same time not detracting from the inherent surface qualities.

'ON' DECORATION

The second category, utilizing colour, can further be subdivided into 'in' and 'on' categories. In this instance the differences refer to whether colouring agents are added to the clay or glaze, or applied directly to a surface. Naturally occurring clays with different body colours (for example, terracotta and porcelain) can be applied in the form of slips to contrast with or compliment the body colour of the ware. Metal oxides can be used directly as pigments, painted on or under glazes, or to provide colour to otherwise lacklustre slips. Some such oxides are used in the form of lustres.

Traditionally, colour techniques have been considered discreet – for example, early English slipware, majolica ware and the high-fired stoneware of the Far East. In Faenza, northern Italy, the original faience techniques, sometimes referred to as majolica ware, are still being taught today. As the popularity of tin-glazed earthenware expanded in Europe, the character of the original faience technique changed to include modelled decoration, as on stoneware. More fluid glazes were then combined with smooth and low-relief surfaces, and matt glazes were used alongside shiny ones, these often being blended together. Rutile and titanium oxide were used widely in addition to tin oxide so that the original nature of the faience tended to get lost. This example illustrates both the tendency

Fig 88   'On' decoration, ranging from slip to lustre ware.

towards innovation on the one hand, and the need to conserve the best traditions on the other. The exciting colour and texture of David White's majolica wares are an indication of how an individual potter has combined two traditional processes to produce an idiosyncratic whole (*see* colour plates and Chapter 10).

SLIP

Earliest forms of pottery from Asia Minor and Mesopotamia (*c*5000BC) relied on white liquid clays painted on to red bodies for decoration. This form of slip-decorated ware has emerged in many cultures throughout history and is still produced by some cultures today. A modern example is the superb pottery produced by the Pueblo Indians of North America, identifiable by strong, simple

forms and bold geometric designs of coloured slips painted directly on to the pots, these being allowed to dry and then burnished with the aid of a smooth pebble or the back of a spoon. Burnishing the surface compresses the small, fine surface particles of clay, hence producing a shine. This ware is unglazed, and has good form and pattern, the contrasts between clay body and/or slips forming a major part in the success of the ware. The Peruvian-inspired dish by Flora Hughes-Stanton (*see* colour plates and Chapter 10) makes use of a similar slip-painting technique.

Slips are very versatile. They may be sprayed, poured, painted, or trailed on to clay surfaces, or a combination of all of these can be used. The consistency will vary according to the type of process used. In addition, you may feel you would like to experiment with colour. A basic white slip that uses 100 per cent white earthenware clay can be changed with the addition of varying percentages of metal oxides or body stains. Your experiments might produce ten different blues, greens or pinks. Please note, however, that you must avoid using copper carbonate or copper oxide slips on internal surfaces of containers that will be used for food (bowls and plates) if they are to be covered with a fritted lead glaze.

COLOURING ADDITIONS

3% Iron oxide	Tan
7% Iron oxide	Brown
1–2% Cobalt oxide	Blue
1–2% Copper carbonate	Green

Body stains Percentages vary with each colour, but 10% is a useful starting point (except for strong colours such as mazarine blue, where they should be used in the same percentage as oxides). For very dense black and red, the following recipes will be useful:

Black slip	**Red slip**
70% Red clay	85% Red clay
15% Manganese	15% Iron oxide
15% Cobalt oxide	

Slips are applied directly on to soft to leather-hard clays. If you wish to paint patterns, sketch your ideas roughly on paper first. A complex pattern will need patience and persistence. A simple but effective starting point could come from geometric shapes such as squares, circles or triangles. See how many permutations you can come up with.

Once you have some idea of pattern, you may begin painting slips on to the surface of your pot (apply two layers). You might find it helpful to mark a few boundary lines lightly to make your job easier. Once the pot and slip become leather hard, you might leave the piece to finish drying out completely or burnish it with the back of a teaspoon. Rub the teaspoon lightly over the surface in a circular motion, taking care not to smear the slip.

Slip Trailing

Slip can also be trailed on to damp or leather-hard clay. Examples of English slipware can be seen in many museums, perhaps the most important being the large platters created by the Toft family during the 18th century.

Slip trailing requires a steady hand, confidence and a bit of practice – try using sheets of newspaper before committing your ideas to clay. The most important tip for success in slip trailing lies in getting the slip to the correct consistency: too runny and your pattern will spread, too thick and the slip will not flow easily out of the slip trailer and will stand too proud of the surface. Don't be afraid to experiment.

Characteristic Properties of Slip

As slips are usually applied to relatively soft, raw clay, there is an immediacy, spontaneity and life inherent in most processes which use slips. Trailed marks or gestures will lend vitality and variety to the decoration, while the studied mixing and control of precise colour provide a complimentary stability to the whole. While it is virtually impossible, and undesirable, to reproduce exactly a lively mark, consistency can be achieved through colour.

Trailing into a ground of slip of a contrasting colour probably allows for the most attractive finished result. The trailed slip tends to settle down into the wet surface, avoiding uncomfortable raised surfaces where they might not be suitable – as on plates. *Gentle* tapping (of the whole piece, on to a bench for example) encourages this settling in of the slip or slips. There are, however, at least a couple of potential problems with the method.

An excess of water contained in the slip can cause the recipient vessel to split or sag. Teapots, jugs and mugs would be at risk where the weight of spouts and handles imposes a downward pull on soggy bodies. Where it is necessary to apply slip to the inside of a piece, pouring usually gives the smoothest result. This should be carried out quickly to prevent sagging, allowing little or no time for moisture to affect the leather-hard clay. Similarly, for exterior applications dip the piece quickly and, if necessary, apply heat and draught to avoid over-wetting. In fact, a hair-drier or electric paint-stripper can be used to stiffen up suspect areas quickly, including handles and spouts, and can be used to hasten the drying of wet slip before further colour is applied. This can prevent the overfamiliar sight of collapsed pots, soggy, detached handles and other associated disasters that can confront you on your return from a well-earned coffee break. Much the same is true when applying glaze prior to once-firing, so a similar ordered procedure is required.

It will also be found that different application processes will demand different slip consistencies. A rather runny, single-cream mix that is suitable for dipping or perhaps painting will probably be too liquid to be trailed successfully. For trailing the consistency will need to be more akin to double cream: thick enough not to spread out excessively, but mobile enough to be used in a slip trailer as mentioned above. To these minor practical problems there are no pat answers, but by trial and error you will soon develop expertise appropriate to your circumstances, finding your own solutions and being rewarded in the knowledge that you did it your way.

The major argument for using slip is its inherent control of colour. Adding known and recorded amounts of oxides to known amounts of dry clay powder will produce consistently predictable results. The same also applies to colouring glazes, while other means of applying oxides to wares are less precise, relying much more on feel and experience. The only requirement for slip is that it is applied evenly; a smooth, rich covering will be achieved, this being further enriched by a transparent, honey or 'iron spangles' glaze.

Conventional and Unconventional Treatments

What follows is an attempt to indicate traditional usage of slip and ways the medium can be used in a more relaxed manner. Similar approaches have been suggested for other techniques so that you can become familiar with a wide range of possibilities which can be used discreetly or in combination. The resulting freedom from convention will allow full rein for creative expression based on traditional expertise and knowledge of the skills involved.

Trailing is possible using plastic squeezy bottles, balloons filled with a glass pipette or, more usually, standard slip trailers bought from any potter's supply shop. The latter come in a range of shapes and sizes, although you may find the smaller slip trailers are sufficient and more comfortable in the hand. Different trailers will have slightly differing nozzle apertures. Should you require a smaller trailed line, a glass pipette can be inserted into the hole of a slip trailer with a removable nozzle, or you can try using the insulation casing from electrical wire as this seems to fit well into the tip of most trailers. As stated earlier, the thickness of trailed lines will also, to some extent, vary according to the consistency of the slip.

Fig 89 Pipette with electrical wire inserted together with other slip trailers.

Before you begin any slip-trailed pattern, you must ensure that your trailers are full. To do this, expel all the air within the bulb, push the tip into the slip and let go. Slip will immediately be taken up into the body of the trailer. When the bulb is re-inflated, extract the tip from the slip, right the bulb and gently squeeze out the excess air until the slip appears at the nozzle. Many pots are ruined because a slip trailer that is half full of air has been used – this causes slip to be spattered out rather than expelled smoothly. Care must be taken not to let air back into the trailer during the decorating process if unwanted spattering is to be avoided. Gentle, steady pressure and a more or less vertical slip railer will help the whole process along.

A simple feathered pattern is a good exercise to begin with. You may wish to try it out on a tile or

Fig 90 Feathering a slipped dish.

scrap of clay first. Begin by either spraying, pouring or painting a base slip on to your dish, then trail two different colours alternately across the surface. Draw the tip of a needle or feather through the lines in one direction, then the other. All that remains is to give the dish a gentle tap or two to allow the slips to flatten and merge together.

Other decorative patterns can be developed by trailing lines of coloured slips in free-swirling patterns. You may wish to experiment in order to develop your own patterns, or be guided initially by historical influences. Much can be gained by research into the trailing techniques of the slip-ware potters of Staffordshire (1600–1700), in addition to those of other cultures.

Marbling

Slips may be used in a variety of ways. Another simple but extremely effective slip technique is that of marbling, which is particularly effective when combined with press moulding as the mould ensures that the dish is well supported throughout the process.

The slab of clay is laid into a suitable press mould. Two to three different coloured slips are then poured on to the surface. Take care not to use excessive amounts of slip for three reasons: it can make the dish oversoft, causing it to dislodge itself from the mould when the surplus is poured off; it can be difficult to get rid of enough slip, thereby causing the clay to become overwet and so crack in the mould during the drying process; and this will be a waste of materials as the eventual mixture of two to three slips is discarded. You will become confident with what amounts to use as you gain experience.

The slips are then swirled and jiggled into patterns by rolling and turning the mould around until

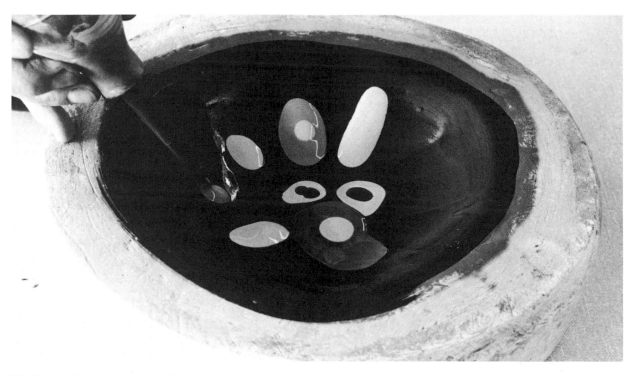

Fig 91 Marbling: (a) pouring slip on to an already slipped dish.

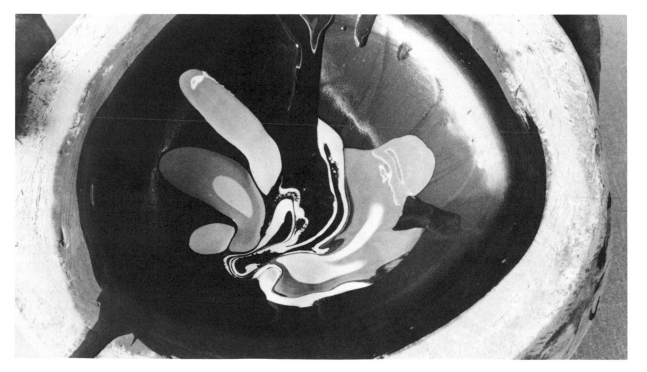

(b) beginning to intermix.

a suitable pattern is effected. The excess slip is then poured out and the rim wiped clear. This simple technique provides a decoration of endless possibilities as no two dishes are ever the same, especially as the possible colour variations are virtually endless with both oxide- and body-stained slips. This technique is also possible on thrown ware, in both flat and vessel form, the latter needing more skill and practice. After biscuit-firing, use either a transparent or honey glaze fired to 1,060–1,100°C.

ENGOBES

The term engobe is often used interchangeably with slip. Essentially, one could use either in similar circumstances, the difference being their composition. Slips are mainly composed of clay, whereas an engobe will contain minerals normally found in glazes. In this way engobes lie somewhere between a slip and a glaze. They provide a vitreous

(c) pouring off any excess.

(d) cleaning up.

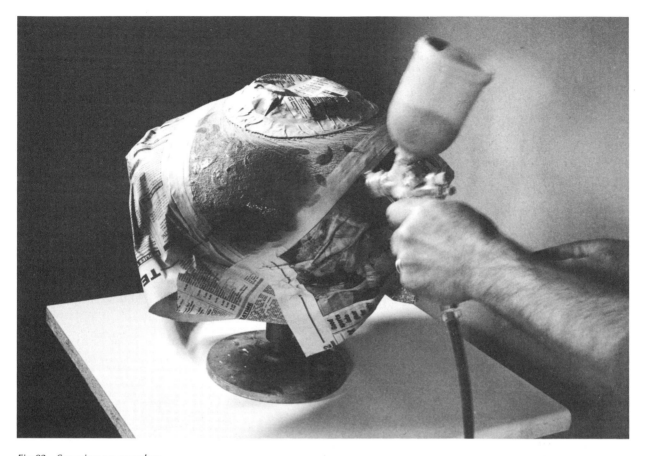

Fig 92 Spraying on engobes.

surface – not at all like the slightly powdery feel of unglazed slipware – which can partly or completely obscure the colour of the original clay body.

As with the slips mentioned above, the colour range of engobes is seemingly endless, with the addition of body stains and oxides. Engobes can be made to suit a range of wares and firing temperatures. The recipe given below for white engobe works well at both earthenware and stoneware temperatures, and is applied to leather-hard clay. Engobes can be dipped, sprayed or painted, or the three techniques can be combined.

If pieces are to be dipped, the consistency of the engobe should be that of a thick glaze, whereas a thicker mix (yoghurt consistency) will be necessary for painting. You will find brushing with engobe easier than with a purely clay-based slip as the engobe seems to catch on the pot, sticking to it quite easily. This is particularly noticeable on a

WHITE ENGOBE	
China clay	25%
Ball clay (Hymod SMD)	25%
Potash feldspar	20%
Flint	20%
Zirconium oxide	5%
Borax frit	5%

Note You may leave out the zirconium oxide for dark colours.

highly grogged clay, where the engobe is a joy to use.

Using Engobes with Brushes

If you intend to use the engobe as a base on which to decorate further with engobes (or oxides), you

Fig 93 Brushing on engobes.

may wish to spray or dip the piece first. That said, engobes brush on just as well and usually cover in two coats with little trouble. Large, flat, Japanese Hake brushes hold good quantities of colour and are ideal for the job.

When painting engobes, wax out any areas you want to remain clear – this is useful if you wish to avoid wiping splashes off foot-rings and the like. Charge your brush fully and paint; when the brush begins to drag, recharge and paint again. Once you have a full base coat, wait for it to become matt before applying a second coat. You may wish to apply more than one colour at either stage. Interesting effects may be achieved if you brush different colours over each other to create soft, overlapping edges. When the engobe dries to leather hard, you could then introduce sgraffito or brush oxides finely on to the surface to introduce further depth.

SGRAFFITO

The traditional approach to sgraffito is to coat a red earthenware body with a suitable white slip. This can be achieved by painting on about three coats of slip, allowing each coat to dry partially (wait until the shiny wet surface has gone matt) before applying the next, brushing at right angles to the previous coat to avoid obvious brushmarks later. Alternatively, take advantage of the chance to lay down a variegated textural surface by being freer with your brush technique. The white coating is then scratched or carved through as the design dictates to reveal the warm red body beneath.

Experiment with coats at different stages of the drying-out process to discover the specific characteristics of different tools and techniques. While the applied coat is still wet (shiny), combing can be effected by dragging appropriate tools lightly

Fig 94 Combing.

through the slip to break its surface. Bold, spontaneous marks can be made using two or three
fingers in unison to wave and zigzag into the wet
surface. You could also try using bristles from a
sweeping brush or the spreader from ceramic-tile
adhesive.

As the surface stiffens, decoration becomes
more studied. Clay removed from the coating and,
possibly, from the body has to be lifted clear of the
tacky surface to prevent unwanted swarf building
up or dropping into the pristine surface pattern.
Various tools are useful: wooden modelling tools;
wire-hooped sculptor's tools; hair grips, possibly
attached to pieces of dowel or old paintbrush
handles. Take care not to allow a build-up of scrap
to clog the tool or spoil the decoration.

If the coating of slip is allowed to dry thoroughly
with its parent body it can be sgraffitoed in the
truest sense, literally by scratching. Where some of

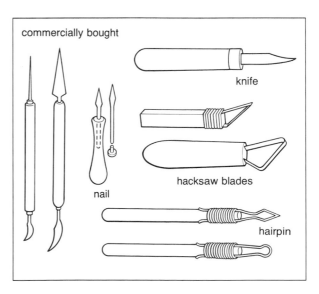

Fig 95 Sgraffito tools can be home-made by modifying
everyday items or materials.

the spontaneity is lost at this stage perhaps, there is ample opportunity for control and fine detail, although there is a tendency for the slip to chip, so cut rather than scratch and use sharp tools. Previously prepared surface-pattern designs can be applied directly from detail or tracing paper on to the dry surface, or can be drawn straight on to the white surface using charcoal or a soft pencil. Light washes of vegetable pigment (coloured inks) could be brushed on to guide your sgraffito tool in cutting away the final design.

Sgraffito tools can, of course, be purchased, and usually come in the form of a double-ended weapon. A sharp point at one end is complemented by a broad but sharp blade at the other. You may find that you can make use of anything as a substitute, from nails ground down into appropriate tools to the misappropriation of lino-cutters or scalpels. The most important feature is that the tools are sharp, and a comfortable grip will also be most welcome if a lot of slip needs to be removed.

Dust and waste needs to be removed regularly from the work surface to keep a clear view of the overall design. It is very tempting to blow away the debris, but as this will only make more cleaning work later, either carefully tip the waste into a suitable receptacle or have a mini vacuum cleaner to hand. Any remaining pencil or wash guidelines will burn away in the biscuit-firing.

An extra dimension can be added to sgraffito by a subsequent addition of oxides and/or body stains. Depending on the exact effect desired, dry stains in powder form can be dusted, brushed, dabbed on with a powder puff, sprinkled or sponged on to and into the surface of the slip coating, either before or after sgraffito, or in combinations.

Oxides can be used raw, where they are applied dry or as water-based washes. On damp surfaces, possibly disturbed by the process of applying oxides, there will normally be a blending with the receiving surface. On a completely dry surface, however, it is advisable to mix up a simple underglaze 'paint' which will assist in binding the oxide to the surface. An addition of a small amount of glaze will provide both vehicle and adhesive, and will also ensure a good bonding with body and glaze when fired later.

Underglaze decoration has a wetted-out look, enhancing colour quality and rendering it entirely permanent, protected by the glaze, and is usually applied to biscuit ware prior to glazing. The procedure for sgraffito and underglaze therefore is first to apply the slip ground to the leather-hard ware, allowing time for it to matt or dry according to when you carve out the design. When this stage of the work is finished, the piece is allowed to dry thoroughly before being fired. The biscuit-ware decoration can then be worked into with underglaze colours, these being mixed with water to a watercolour consistency. Transparent glaze is then applied over the whole piece by dipping, pouring or spraying, and firing takes place again. Pots decorated in this way benefit from the strength of the sgraffitoed line, coupled with the soft fluidity of the underglaze colours. Additionally, the underglaze painting technique works well on a ground of white slip without the sgraffitoed line.

Fig 96 Brushing dry underglaze colour on to damp slip.

Fig 97 'Washing' underglaze colour on to biscuit-fired decoration.

ALTERNATIVE TECHNIQUES

Some years ago I was intrigued to watch a potter throw a simple cylinder, then, while it was still wet on the wheel, cover it with white powder. (Any white powder would do – feldspar, whiting, china clay – so long as it provided a good covering and was ceramic in origin.) He then proceeded to transform the cylinder into a spherical teapot body by using a padded rib on a stick, rather like a boxing glove. This was used to widen the vessel from within, leaving the outside untouched. As the wet clay stretched, it caused the dry outer layer to craze, giving the form a remarkable crackle texture. With considerable dexterity – and showmanship, it must be said – he then used similar principles to manufacture the lid, spout and handle to complete the piece.

Variations on Printing Principles

By experimenting with oxides, body stains and rough surfaces, colour and texture can be rendered on to slabs before they are pressed into or over moulds or formers. Pigment can be picked up, having been previously lightly and arbitrarily dusted on to a flat surface – usually a dry, absorbent wooden board. The partially flattened lump of clay in hand can be rolled out to the desired thickness so that oxides or body stains (or both) adhere to the clay, and then, after stretching, break to create chance texture and colour staining. Reverse texture can similarly be impressed into slabs from a wide range of surfaces; try rough-sawn wood, bricks, plastic or rubber matting.

In a similar way, pigment can be printed by offsetting on to the clay surface:

Fig 98 (a–b)   Picking up colour and texture from an oxide-dusted and heavily textured piece of wood. (c) dry feldspar coating 'stretched' to produce a fissured texture.

Step 1 Colour is applied to old newspaper on a flat surface.

Step 2 A slab is rolled out to almost the desired thickness on a separate cloth.

Step 3 The slab and cloth supporting it are then inverted on to the wet design and newspaper.

Step 4 After removing the cloth, the slab is rolled out to the desired thickness.

Step 5 A board is placed over the slab, and both boards are then picked up with the clay and paper sandwiched between them.

Step 6 The board and newspaper are removed to reveal a printed image offset on to the slab.

Step 7 The slab is installed into the piece as required. If the newsprint breaks up in the process, leave the bits *in situ* as they will burn away in the biscuit-firing. Sugar paper or cartridge paper can be used if a more durable support is required.

The above will not produce a high-definition image and final statement, rather it will provide an underpainting, texture and a starting point for further action at different stages in the development of the ware. At best it can act as a springboard; at worst it could be sponged or scraped off.

A more sophisticated result is often possible by making use of the monoprinting technique, or rather a slight variation on it. The basic principle is similar to that of carbon paper:

Step 1 Coat newsprint or old newspaper with heavily stained slip; several coatings may be required, and one or more colours can be used.

Step 2 When the slip surface has become matt, invert the sheet on to the pot so the slipped surface is in contact with the clay. Now, by drawing on the paper, slip will be deposited on to the slab.

Fig 99 Monoprinting: (a) coating newspaper with slip.

(b) invert on to a slab.

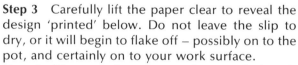

(c) draw (or trace) on to the newspaper.

(d) the monoprint.

Step 3 Carefully lift the paper clear to reveal the design 'printed' below. Do not leave the slip to dry, or it will begin to flake off – possibly on to the pot, and certainly on to your work surface.

Step 4 Dispose of any unused paper before it dries so as to avoid the health and safety hazard of spreading flaking slip.

Designs can be prepared on detail or tracing paper prior to printing. From the original artwork, the printing can be carried out in two alternative ways:

Method A

Step 1 Prepare the pot and 'carbon paper' as above.

Step 2 Lay the artwork on top of the blank, upper side of the newsprint.

Step 3 Trace over the original. A little more pressure will be needed to obtain a clean print, which may in any case not be quite as crisp as the direct approach above.

Method B

Step 1 Transfer the design on to newsprint *before* coating the reverse side with slip.

Step 2 When the newsprint is then placed *in situ* on the slab, your design can simply be redrawn on to the pot.

The resulting line-drawing which has been transferred on to the clay may be sufficient as a decoration. It can also provide a useful 'clothesline' on which to build up richer, more complex designs by brushing or spraying on further slips or underglaze colours. With care, it is also possible to super-impose further monoprints, but consideration must be given to the problems of offsetting (lifting off some of the work that has already been done) and the drying-out process.

Note When monoprinting, avoid impressing marks in the clay by tracing just firmly enough to deposit slip on to the surface of the slab. Try not to have contact of any sort with the 'carbon paper' or tracing otherwise unwanted marks will appear on the slab. As the slip coating dries out completely, it will no longer be usable. Dispose of it carefully to prevent unnecessary dust in the workshop as the dry slip flakes off.

Slip and Wax

Patterns can be created as stated earlier by painting slips directly on to wet or leather-hard clay surfaces. A negative effect to this can be created by painting wax or wax emulsion directly on to the leather-hard surface and then spraying or brushing slip over this. The wax will reject the slip, leaving the background slipped and the pattern as bare clay. This could be further enhanced with the occasional well-placed slip-trailed dot or line to give the design a second dimension. A word of warning: if wax emulsion is used, wait until it dries on the surface of the clay (this applies to biscuit pots too) as the slip or glaze will stick to the wet emulsion and you will be no better off.

This technique can be used on both earthenware and stoneware pots (providing the slip will go up to stoneware temperatures). Particularly effective is a blue slip on a stoneware clay fired and covered with a dolomite or gloss-white glaze.

Glaze and Wax

Wax will resist glaze in the same way as slip, thereby affording further opportunity to create exciting surface patterns. Where wax is brushed on to biscuit ware, that part of the surface will remain unglazed after firing. This is therefore not a good choice at earthenware temperatures, but is particularly effective at stoneware.

The double-dipping method is suitable for both earthenware and stoneware. The piece is fully glazed with a first glaze. Wax is then used to apply decoration to the dry surface of the glaze, either applied in bold brush strokes or splashed on. A second contrasting glaze is then applied. The colour of the first glaze will be evident after firing in the waxed areas, while the remaining areas will be a combination of both glazes. To retain an area of the usual colour of the second glaze, it would be necessary to prevent the first glaze from covering all the unwaxed biscuit surface; wax cannot be used because it would also reject the second glaze. This suggests that you should either not glaze all

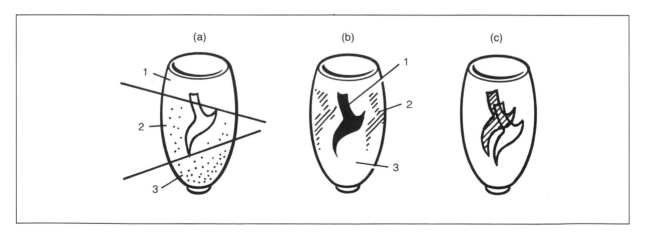

Fig 100 Masking and double glazing.
(a) double-dipped with painted on oxide decoration.
   (i) angled dip – first glaze.
   (ii) other end dipped.
   (iii) centre section with overlapping glazes.

(b) (i) masked prior to first glaze application.
   (ii) adhesive mask over glaze.
   (iii) remaining areas receive all applications.
(c) apply adhesive or paper mask before first glaze is applied. Second and/or subsequent glaze/stains are sprayed through the stencil.

Fig 101   (a) using a stencil to mask spray of application of slip.

(b) carefully removing adhesive 'mask'.

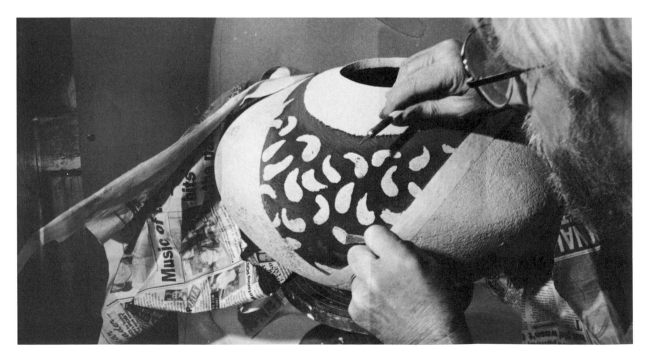

(c) the finished result.

over the piece in the first place, or instead use some other form of removable resist or stencil to protect those areas that are to remain free of the first glaze. Simple torn or cut paper stencils can be stuck temporarily to the biscuit ware using a little water to dampen the paper. After glazing, the paper can be removed to expose that part of the ware that is to receive only the second application of glaze. This technique is also suitable for the spray application of glaze.

An interesting alternative to this method is to use a latex-rubber-based adhesive such as Copydex. This can be applied in the same way as wax, but can be peeled off carefully later on. With ingenuity and planning it is possible to maximize on both permutations of colour and texture when creative combinations of these techniques are exploited.

The resist/rejection principle is often made use of by potters who wish to prevent glaze taking on parts of a piece likely to be in contact with either the kiln bat or other components such as lids. Such areas can be given a protective coating of wax emulsion to avoid the need for cleaning off glaze later. This saves time and effort that might be better used elsewhere.

Stencils

These can be used in conjunction with other processes or independently to mask out areas that are to remain free of colour. Either a positive or negative image can be made by cutting or tearing paper. Both the outer and inner paper shapes can be used as a mask, or the two can be combined to create random superimpositions, patterns and textures.

Various application techniques can be used with stencils. Slip, underglaze colours or any other ceramic decoration material can be stippled, painted, sprayed, spattered (with a toothbrush), sponged or printed on to the surface. This can be

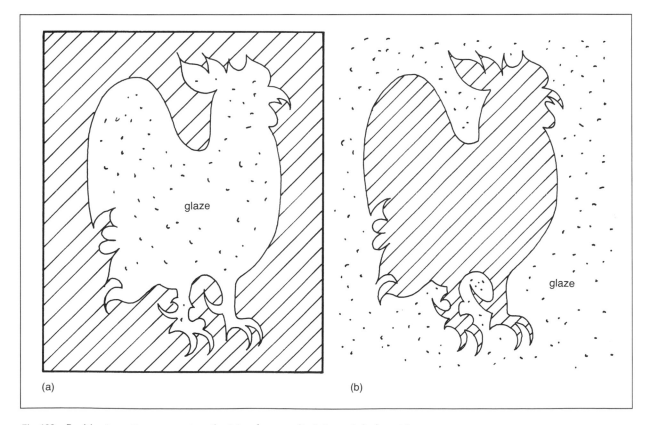

(a)   (b)

Fig 102   Positive/negative paper stencils. (a) colour applied through hole cut in paper.
(b) colour applied to background.

done at any stage of the overall ceramic process. At an early stage, oxides could be sprayed or painted on to wet clay, while at a late stage enamels or lustres could be applied after the glaze-firing.

Search for novel material to use as stencils; the ubiquitous leaf serves to illustrate the idea, but it does fall firmly into the cliché file. Remember that the first application of colour will in all probability be only the start, a foundation on which to build further with varied applications and techniques. So, if a piece of plastic netting seems somewhat prosaic, bear in mind that it is what happens later which turns it into poetry. Experiment with paper doilies, lace curtains, or anything else that will provide a protective mask and give rise to an interesting visual result.

Large stencils of a complex nature are only suitable for one-offs as they will inevitably become sodden and unmanageable after use. Smaller versions could be used on a scale suitable for short runs of tiles, particularly if stencil material is carefully matched to the decorating medium – a thick paper or card will not be reduced to a soggy apology too soon if used with a relatively stiff slip. Simple shapes with no fiddly, thin apertures will be easier

to handle than extremely detailed cut-outs. On a small scale, and if a simple motif is to be used, it might not be unacceptable to make several identical stencils to increase the number of prints possible. However, if the task in hand is worth the effort, why not attempt silk-screen printing instead?

Silk-Screen Printing

This can only be carried out on a flat surface, which restricts opportunities to the following:

- Printing directly on to clay.
- Printing directly on to glaze (fired or not). Only tiles can be decorated.
- Indirect printing via transfers.

The process, as its name implies, makes use of silk as a support for a stencil. Silk, or one of the numerous specialist man-made fibres available, is stretched across a rectangular frame to form a tympan in much the same way as a canvas is stretched prior to painting. The nature of the material will allow paint or ink to pass through. A stencil attached to the back of the screen will prevent

Fig 103   Printing on to a slab of plastic clay.

passage of ink except where the silk is exposed – in other words, not blocked by the stencil. In this way the colouring medium can be forced repeatedly through the mesh to leave a printed image on numerous individual pieces, depending only on the type of stencil used. It is not intended here to give in-depth technical details of specialist silk-screen processes as simple paper stencils will usually suffice for basic ceramic situations. However, where a more detailed or long-lasting stencil is required, it would be best to paint out the silk as described below.

Making and Preparing a Screen

You can either make a screen for use on tiles from recycled material (for example, a picture frame or small window frame minus the glass), or create a custom-designed and built item from 1 × 1in (2.5 × 2.5cm) planed timber. The screen may be constructed from either softwood or hardwood, and can be 6 × 6in (15 × 15cm) or 6 × 18in (15 × 20cm). Note the following:

- Joints should be neat and the frame should rest completely flat when laid on a work surface.
- Outer edges should be chamfered off to allow the material to stretch around the screen frame without snagging.

Now stretch a piece of fabric over the frame (a piece of silk is ideal):

Step 1 Lay the material flat on a smooth, clean surface.
Step 2 Place the frame on top of the material so that there is at least 2in (5cm) spare for wrapping around the timber.
Step 3 Tack one side of the silk to the tip of the frame, then pull gently but firmly at the opposite side at right angles to the frame, ensuring that the

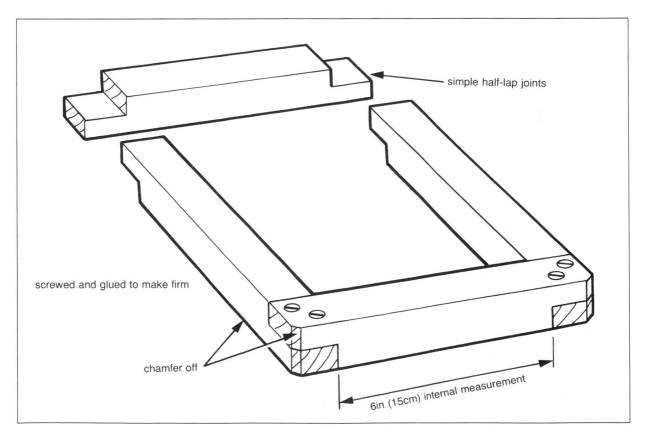

simple half-lap joints

screwed and glued to make firm

chamfer off

6in (15cm) internal measurement

Fig 104   Construction of a silkscreen frame.

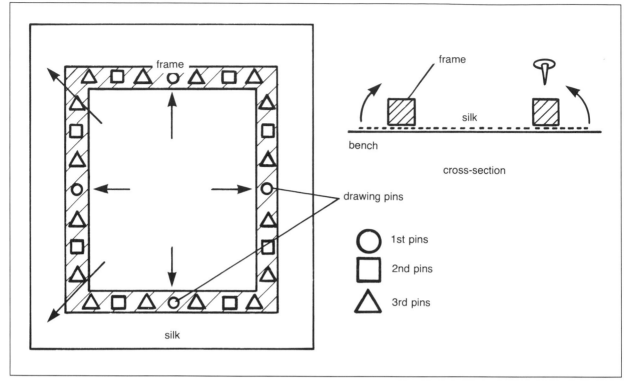

Fig 105　Stretching the silk.

pressure is directly along the warp or weft. Work on the length first if it is rectangular.

Step 4　Next, stretch the material across the width in the same way – at the half-way point.

Step 5　Using a sides-to-middle system, fasten the material down at the quarter-way points, taking care to apply some diagonal outward pull in order to avoid built-in slackness when fixing the other sides.

Step 6　The corners can be eased outward and up, forming a neat fold that is fastened down when the material is seen to be flat and straight.

Step 7　Fasten down at the midpoints in any gaps, easing out any minor sagginess without over-stressing the silk. Final fastenings will need to be about 1in (2.5cm) apart.

Step 8　The silk should now be perfectly flat with little or no movement when pressed gently; in fact, it should be almost as tight as a drumskin.

On the suggested scale you will probably have little difficulty getting a good screen stretched at your first attempt. However, larger screens tend to be a little more difficult. You may find that drawing-pins can be used initially to set the material more or less in place, removing them and applying a little extra tension before final fixing with either drawing-pins or an impact staple gun. The completed silk screen is now ready to receive its stencil.

Fabric under tension is obviously prone to damage. If care is taken to avoid this and the screen is cleaned thoroughly after use, it will last for years. If only simple paper cut-out stencils are used, the screen need only ever have contact with a squeegee, some sort of paint (slip and the like) and water when washed. If a stencil is made by painting out parts of the fabric (to block off areas) it will have to be either cleaned off with an appropriate solvent or discarded. As most ceramic printing is likely to be water based, this painting-out would have to use either an oil-based or insoluble acrylic paint; an old tin of unwanted household gloss paint will be perfectly adequate, although it may require a second coat to eliminate 'pin-holes'. If a piece of second-hand material can be found at a jumble sale, it will hardly matter anyway if the screen is subsequently destroyed.

Preparing the Stencil

This is very straightforward in theory, although in practice there may be one or two minor problems.

If a hole is cut in a sheet of newsprint, and the paper supported by the screen, then there is no problem. If part of the stencil is cut completely from its parent piece, however, it will have to be positioned carefully prior to attachment to the screen. It would not be difficult to do so on a simple template, but with a complex design containing a great many unattached pieces it might be very time-consuming if not almost impossible to get all the pieces in place. Do not forget that random designs, picking up arbitrarily scattered pieces, might be an interesting alternative to a considered complex and formal design.

A reasonable solution to the difficulty illustrated can be reached by compromise. The design can be modified to give support to otherwise loose elements, and the stencil cut accordingly as follows:

Step 1 When the outline design is drawn or transferred on to the thin paper, the stencil can be cut out using a scalpel or craft knife. Support the paper on a sheet of thick card or hardboard to protect the work surface and carefully cut away unwanted paper. Before cutting, make sure that the paper stencil is large enough to allow the excess to be folded up and taped to the outside of the frame.

Step 2 Lay the screen down on to the stencil, fold up and tape in place. The design should be more or less centred within the frame with some masked border all round, but particularly at two opposite ends.

Step 3 Place the screen in place upon a slab of clay, and add printing medium (slip, etc) across the space left at one end of the screen.

Step 4 Use a squeegee to draw slip across the design to the opposite end of the screen, lift squeegee over the slip and return, again dragging the slip to its original side. (Slip used for screen printing has to be very fine: at least a 120-mesh sieve will be needed to prepare the slip.)

Step 5 Lift the frame, with slip and squeegee *in situ*, off the slab, placing it down with the slip-containing end slightly raised. Use a piece of 2 × 1 in off-cut. This will prevent slip from running back to drip through the screen.

The paper stencil should now have become well attached to the screen by the slip and will be good for at least a dozen or so pulls.

The original design should have been clearly printed off on the leather-hard slab. Check that the consistency is right: too runny and it will bleed back under the stencil, too thick and it will not easily pass through the screen.

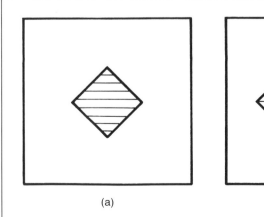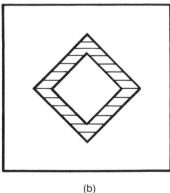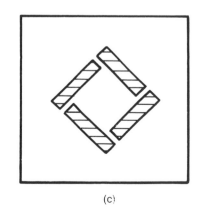

(a)　　　　　　　　(b)　　　　　　　　(c)

Fig 106 (a) simple stencil – a hole in a background. (b) stencil with 'loose' central feature. (c) as above with supporting 'bridges' connecting and supporting centre feature.

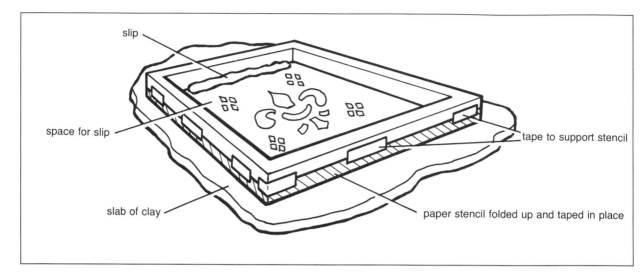

Fig 107 Stencil located within screen area, taped to frame.

Ready-prepared slabs can now be printed either pre-cut or trimmed after. Consideration needs to be given to register: that is, ensuring that positioning is reasonably precise. Some form of locating system for tile and frame might be useful. As long as the position of the tile and screen are constant, the stencil can be located on the screen to suit. If you choose to print on to untrimmed slabs, the precise registering of the print is of no account: you will be able to cut the tile to centre the design as required.

If a large screen is available it is possible to print a free, non-figurative surface pattern, having picked up on to the screen assorted shapes as suggested above. With care it is possible to superimpose a second, or even a third colour provided that each is allowed to lose its shine and stiffen sufficiently so that it is not smudged by subsequent contact with the screen. A tile-cutter can then be used to make the most of the decorated slabs, each tile having a unique pattern with intriguing variations while maintaining a unified whole.

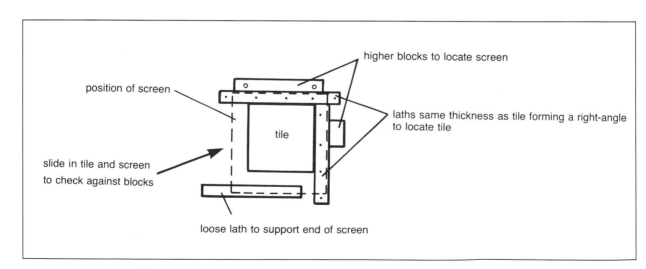

Fig 108 System for locating tile and screen.

Stoneware bowl by John Calver. Diameter 10in (25cm).

Porcelain 'bottle in box' by Sarah Dunstan.

Earthenware jugs, standing 6in (15cm) and 10in (25cm) high, by Victoria and Michael Eden.

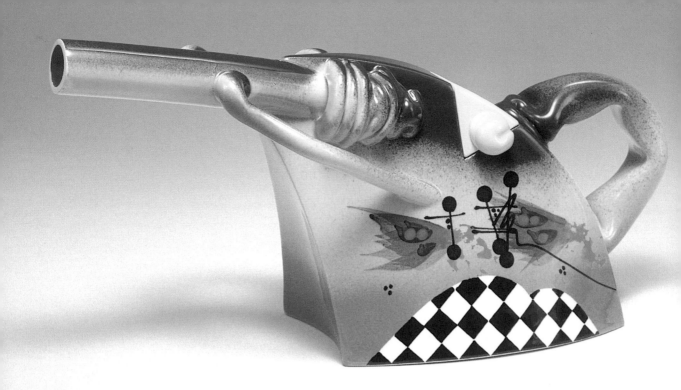

Earthenware teapot by Richard Godfrey.

'Still vessels' by Melanie Hunter. Maximum height is 19in (48cm).

Naked raku vase by Peter Ilsley standing 7in (18 cm) high.

Peter Ilsley used a macro crystalline glaze to brilliant effect on this 8in (21cm) porcelain bottle.

Three dry copper raku vessels, by Peter Ilsley. Maximum height is 7in (18cm).

Earthenware bowls by Flora Hughes-Stanton.
They are 7in (18cm) and 7.25in (20cm) in
diameter respectively.

Will Levi Marshall's unusual 'pink-on-pink' teapot is in enamelled and lustred stoneware.

Stoneware vessel by Carlos van Reigersberg Versluys.

Stoneware teapot by Carlos van Reigersberg Versluys.

Burnished smoke-fired pot by Antonia Salmon. It stands 15in (38cm) high.

Two of Ruthanne Tudball's
creations: (above) a salt-glazed,
faceted teapot, 6.5in (17cm) tall;
and (right) a spouted faceted jug,
also salt glazed, and standing
almost 8in (20cm) high.

A thrown and coiled stoneware pot by Robin Welch.

This unusual earthenware jar by Judith Wensley stands 32in (82cm) high.

A group of earthenware teapots by Judith Wensley.

Stoneware creations by Doug Wensley: (left) a sculptural form standing almost 20in (50cm) high; and (right) a tall form standing 22in (55cm) high.

Earthenware teapot by David White.

A brief note on squeegees. Professionally made items can be purchased, but home-made versions are relatively simple to construct. Where it is intended only to work at about a 4–6in (10–15cm) width, you may well find that either a car-windscreen-cleaning squeegee (possibly reduced in length) or even a piece of stiff cardboard will be adequate. For short runs and/or when using expensive oxides, it might be more convenient to sponge the pigment through the stencil, or to brush or stipple it. The main aim is to repeat the print; if you are not sticking to the silk-screen rules it really does not matter. A mini-squeegee can be made from a short piece of windscreen-wiper blade supported on a piece of flat wood.

Printing on to Fired Ware

The most convenient method is to print on to biscuit with underglaze colour, applying a transparent glaze after. Printing on to a glazed but unfired surface with on-glaze colour involves matching ink and a dry, dusty surface. If you need to print long runs it would help if you harden on the glaze first by firing up to 800–1,000°C; this consolidates the surface, enhancing absorbency so that on-glaze colour is more readily accepted. It is a process used in some commercial potteries to provide a better base for on-glaze painting, its main drawbacks being that if mistakes are made they cannot be wiped off or easily disguised, and costs are

increased by the addition of an extra firing and with all the handling that entails.

By mixing up a suitable 'paint', it is possible to print directly on to a fired-glaze surface, given that it is flat. As a minor warpage would create major problems when using a silk screen direct, and as mixing special paint is necessary, the logical solution is to create transfers.

Transfers

These are underglaze and on-glaze decorations applied indirectly. Ceramic colour motifs are printed on to paper or a flexible plastic base, from which they are transferred on to the surface of the pot. Simple transfers can be made as follows:

Step 1 Use brown gummed paper or ceramic transfer paper for the paper base. Two things are important: the gum should be water-soluble and of good thickness; and the backing paper should be absorbent.

Step 2 The design can be either silk-screen printed, or hand-painted directly on to the surface of the gum using an oil-based medium such as artist's clear varnish or fat oil (made from pure turpentine). Conventional ceramic oxides, on-glaze colours or enamels can also be used, provided that firing temperatures are compatible – in other words, do not mix enamels with oxides on

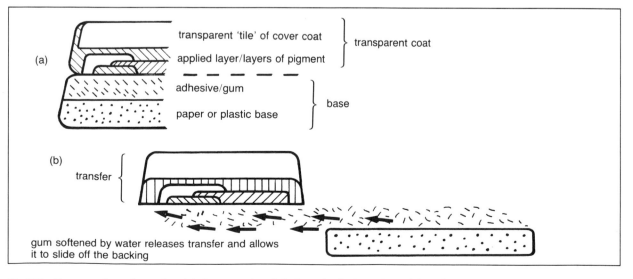

Fig 109   Cross-section of transfer: (a) dry, completed design; (b) design released from base.

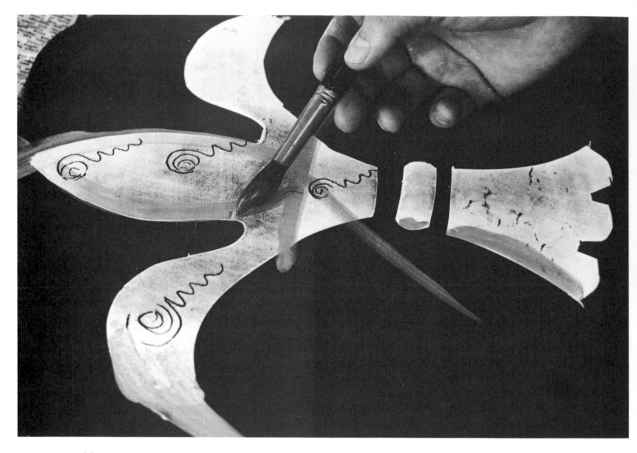

Fig 110   Modifying a screened image.

the same transfer that is intended for firing at a temperature which would burn off either 'soft' oxides or enamels.

Step 3   The completed motif will now require a support, holding all the disparate colours in their correct places. Covercoat, bought from suppliers, will provide this support, and should be applied after sufficient time is allowed for the 'paints' to dry thoroughly – usually about twenty-four hours.

Step 4   When the completed transfer is immersed in water the adhesive on the paper base dissolves. This allows the applied transfer to be slid off its base carefully and placed in position on the pot to be decorated. Considerable care is needed to ensure that no air bubbles are trapped under the transfer. If one corner or edge is positioned first, with the remaining skin curving away from the pot's surface, the whole can be lowered progressively so that air is excluded as the transfer is

brought into contact with the surface. A sponge, squeegee or rubber kidney can sometimes be used to assist the process.

Note the following points:

• As mentioned above, pigments need to be matched to firing temperatures.
• The best procedure is probably to glaze-fire the pot, then apply a transfer using enamel colour that fires at 850°C or so.

Transfer Base Paper

This can be purchased from specialist suppliers in sheet form, is obviously better suited to the process than gummed brown paper, and allows for greater scope in experimentation. Surface pattern can be applied to the base paper by a wide variety of means, including painting, spraying, stencilling,

Fig 111 Transfer decoration.

silk-screen printing, sponging, splattering and so on. Large surface areas can be decorated so that the paper can later be cut up to size. By such means exciting colour, pattern and textural effects can be developed and applied in transfer form to any suitable ceramic surface.

Colouring Pigments

These usually fall into two categories: underglazes and glazes and body stains. Underglaze colours are purchased in powder form for application to either pre-biscuit clay (green hard) or biscuit ware after being mixed into a paint using an appropriate medium purchased from the same supplier. Both medium and pigment must be blended together thoroughly, this being best achieved by using a palette knife to rub the two together on a flat, smooth surface – a glazed tile or piece of plate

glass is ideal. With the addition of 30 per cent or a little more of transparent glaze or frit, these colours can then be applied on raw glaze in the manner of majolica ware. Stains and colours can be made self-glazing, and matt colours developed by adding sufficient amounts of flux.

The normal means of using glaze or body stains is by addition to glazes (5–8 per cent) or slips (10–18 per cent), passing the whole through a 120-mesh sieve later on. As above, glazes and body stains can be used on raw glaze or as underglaze colours if prepared as suggested. However, be sure to check that colours/stains are capable of surviving intended firing temperatures. Manufacturers indicate firing ranges, usually highlighting either those not suited for high temperatures, or those which are.

Colours and stains can, of course, be added directly to a clay body, either sieved into the body at slip consistency to produce an even colouring, wedged in as dry powder to plastic clay to variegate or speckle the body, or by wetting down the body stain with a small amount of boiling water, sieving this mix and then kneading it carefully into the base clay. Used in porcelain or T-material, clean, positive colours can be obtained, enabling a wide range of marbled, inlaid, laminated and agate ware effects to be created. Sculptural pieces built by the author involve the use of stained clays integrated with others that have been textured and mottled by picking up loose, dry stains in the rolling-out processes. More formal pattern and decoration would involve careful trials to test for colour, and extensive development of ideas in a sketch book. Exploration of geometric patterns based on chequer or square units, triangular motifs or more complex interlocking forms would be a good starting point. Conversely, free-formed designs might be developed from drawings, as illustrated in the laminated bowl with swimming figures.

Project – Laminated Bowl

This would appear to be essentially a building project, but its success depends largely on its integrated decoration. The first requirement is a suitable plaster mould; alternatively, make use of a biscuit-fired bowl. Next, prepare a limited range of body-stained coloured clays using one basic body. First attempts will best be based on a white earthenware body which will not be prone to slumping when fired. T-material or porcelain can be used, but, depending on the shape of the finished piece, will require props or other support structures when fired to high temperatures. These coloured bodies can be used individually, laid into the mould as pre-cut shapes, or can be worked into rolls or stratified slabs before being cut and arranged in formal patterns.

Step 1   Line the mould or biscuit-fired bowl with a very thin slab or sheet of white clay.

Fig 112   Laminated bowl.

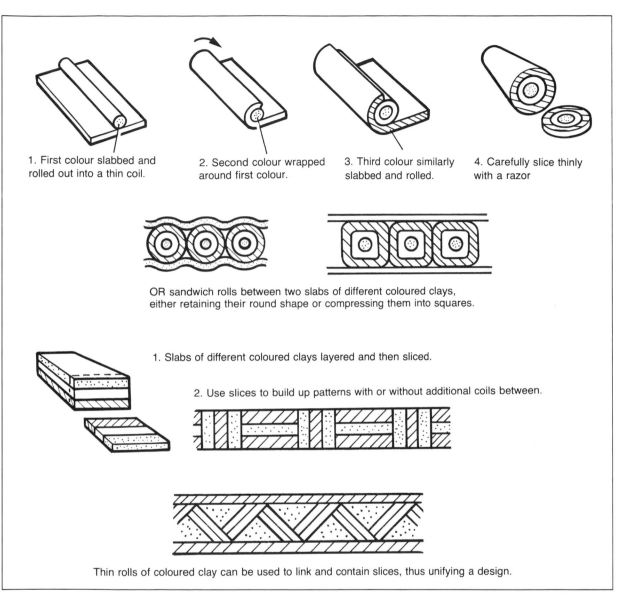

1. First colour slabbed and rolled out into a thin coil.

2. Second colour wrapped around first colour.

3. Third colour similarly slabbed and rolled.

4. Carefully slice thinly with a razor

OR sandwich rolls between two slabs of different coloured clays, either retaining their round shape or compressing them into squares.

1. Slabs of different coloured clays layered and then sliced.

2. Use slices to build up patterns with or without additional coils between.

Thin rolls of coloured clay can be used to link and contain slices, thus unifying a design.

Fig 113 Making pre-formed modules for lamination process.

Step 2 Use dividers or a compass to mark out guide-lines for the proposed design (*see* table below). Horizontal bands will provide a guideline grid on which to build geometric patterns. Verticals will help divide the circular area into equal slices or segments.

Step 3 Begin to apply slices and thin coils (possibly flattened by a rolling pin after hand-rolling) to build up the desired design. Use a sable water-colour brush to apply slip when attaching pieces.

Step 4 When the building process is completed, allow the whole to stiffen until leather hard or even drier. Use a metal kidney to scrape away bumps; this will both ensure a smooth surface and will reveal clean, sharp resolutions to the coloured clays incorporated into the structure.

Step 5 After removing the piece from its supporting mould, the white clay can now be scraped away

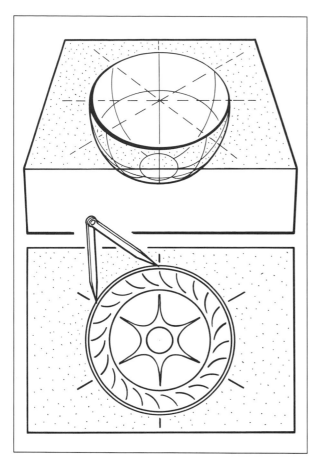

Fig 114 (a) perspective view – mould guidelines
with white clay in place.
(b) use compass or dividers to locate the major
guideline. Mark the plaster with a soft pencil or
oxide, or directly on the pot.

strength to the piece. Completed vessels will have
a relatively uniform outside surface, with an irregular relief pattern on the inside where the clay is not
directly in contact with the supporting mould.

Firing

When porcelain is used in this way to produce
bowl shapes, I have fired them up to 1,300°C, unglazed and placed in an unglazed stoneware-fired
bowl containing fine white sand to act as a supporting cushion. The bodies, being vitrified, have a
satin appearance and are characteristically trans-
lucent if finely constructed.

Geometry

Creating designs within a circle can appear rather
complicated. If divisions are to be more interesting
than quarters and eighths, calculations based
on radius and circumference appear to dampen
enthusiasm. So, if a division into five, seven or
nine segments seems preferable to four or eight
segments, the following may be of use if you have
a simple protractor to hand:

Number of Divisions	1	2	3*	4	5*	6*	7*	8	9*
Size in Degrees (°)	360	180	120	90	72	60	51	45	40

*visually more interesting divisions

When even a protractor is not readily at hand, use
a length of string instead:

Step 1 Cut the string to the length required for it
to wrap round the circle that is to be divided – in
other words, around the belly or rim.
Step 2 With a little patience, this string can now
be folded into the required number of equal
lengths. Use the folded length of string or set the
compass or dividers to mark out the divisions.
 To mark out circles to indicate bands on the
inside of the vessel, either use a compass or band
in guide-lines with a brush, having centred the
vessel in its mould on a wheel, in the same way as
one would decorate the outside of a thrown pot.

carefully using a razor blade or steel kidney to
reveal the design below, this being accentuated by
the remaining incursions of white clay between
coloured bodies.

As an alternative method to the above you could
again use a plaster mould, this time inlaying an
arbitrary design using strips of white body and incorporating coloured images as appropriate. Some
superimposition, possibly suggesting interwoven
strips, will provide some relief surface and additional

7

Unorthodox Procedures

This section briefly outlines a few unconventional procedures which do not fall easily into any of the categories covered elsewhere in this book. They may suggest other procedures to you which, although seeming to contradict conventional craft practices, extend the boundaries of your ceramics experience.

GLAZE

If exciting, accidental or arbitrary texture and pattern are required at the glazing stage, try soaking pieces of open-weave material such as sack cloth in glaze. Next, apply a coat of another glaze to the piece and then apply bits of the glaze-soaked material which will adhere to this base glaze. During the firing process all vegetable matter (in this case the cloth) will burn away, leaving its character and image encapsulated in the remaining glaze. Similarly, strings and wool can be used to build up applied glaze patterns that are impossible to achieve by other means. This technique is suitable only for matt glazes applied to horizontal surfaces.

SLIP

Absorbent materials can also be used to transport or support clays at the building and decorating stages. Possibilities here are virtually limitless – for example, lacy patterns can be applied by laying suitably soaked material on to press-moulded slab dishes, or directly into moulds. Casting slip can be absorbed and allowed to dry out in garments so that after biscuit-firing one is left with, for example, a ceramic T-shirt. As an end in itself, this may have less to offer than as a means of achieving something a little more substantial. However, if it suggests an avenue for exploration it was certainly worth mentioning.

Fig 115 Applying slip-soaked sacking.

CLAY

As mentioned above, clay can be stained. If red clay is an impure clay acceptable for its colour, then local clays containing mineral particles, and so similarly impure, could be described as speckled. Additions of appropriate coarse oxides, metals or refractory substances can be added to bland clay bodies to render them textured or speckled after firing and glazing. Iron filings, stone dust, ceramic chips and all manner of other likely material can be added to enhance the visual appearance of fired bodies. Some impurities simply add extra colour or texture, while others melt in the fire giving rise to eruptions and bursts of colour on the surface of the clay and/or glaze.

In the recent past, combustible matter has also been added to clay. This serves the dual purpose of adding textural interest and lightening the fired piece. Sawdust has been a favourite ingredient, while additions of nylon and glass fibre have also been used. More recently, a more humble and less likely ingredient has been cellulose fibre.

Paper Clay

This is simply a mixture of paper in pulp form and any clay. It has been found that such a mixture will produce a raw material with surprising properties of considerable interest to potters.

Cellulose fibre, a hollow, tube-like structure, is a basic ingredient in plant matter, is therefore a major constituent of paper pulp, and is readily available to potters in the form of paper, waste or otherwise. Tissue paper, newsprint and photo-copying paper are among the most suitable; card-board and specialist papers containing dressings such as kaolin and glues are much less suitable. The hollow fibres in the paper absorb water and will also draw up minute particles of clay. The latter effect results in a complex structure of fibre and clay slip, with amazing and unusual working properties that are of significant consequence to ceramic sculptors in particular.

Mixing the Pulp

Paper need only be torn up and soaked in hot water. Mechanical assistance may, however, be necessary to speed up the process; use an electric drill with a mixer attachment. Use paper that tears easily as it will also soak down quicker than a tough paper. When the pulp is sufficiently mashed down, put it in a kitchen sieve to drain off excess water. This pulp is now ready to be mixed with clay. The most convenient method is to use casting slip. Otherwise, use slop, slurry and/or turnings. Allow the mixture to soak overnight if dry particles are added, and stir to blend it into a smooth, creamy consistency. Blend the two materials together in a

ratio by volume of 10–50 per cent pulp.

Disadvantages

- It is difficult or impossible to throw.
- It is equally disinclined to be kneaded.
- After a couple of weeks it develops a nasty smell, so do not normally mix up more than can be used immediately. Any surplus can be put into plastic bags and frozen, or allowed to dry out (*see* below).

Advantages

- The wet mix can be poured out onto plaster slabs to appropriate thickness and allowed to dry.
- There will be almost no likelihood of major cracking during drying.
- Can be used directly to lay up moulds.
- Can be used for coiling.
- Pieces can be joined at any stage: wet, leather-hard and dry pieces can be joined without prob-lem.
- Incredible tensile strength develops as the material dries.
- Fired pieces can be incorporated with the soft material.
- Strength/weight ratio is increased by up to 50 per cent.
- Dry pieces can be cut using a craft knife or small saw blade, or scored and snapped off over the edge of a table.
- Thoroughly dry slabs or rolls of paper clay can be stored for later use, either used as formed, or
- Can be soaked down to a malleable, leather-hard state by two to three hours' immersion in water.
- Surface texture can be controlled. In its original state it has a porridge-like surface which can be smoothed down using a fine sponge, sand-papered or filed, depending on how dry it has become.

Firing

The material fires exactly as clay, and also looks and behaves like clay because that is what it is. If fired in an electric kiln it is advisable to have both vents and door open, firing up slowly through 300°C up to 500°C. Increase the temperature at about 50° or 70° per hour to burn off the paper fibre and allow smoke to disperse before it becomes an unpleasant hazard. Doors and windows should remain open to allow maximum ventilation. Where fossil fuels are used and kilns are fitted with chimneys, there will be no such·problem. After biscuit-firing, the pieces can be glazed and fired in the conventional way.

This unlikely material offers, in large measure, the sort of freedom this book seeks to encourage.

The chance to build with preformed slabs and sludge, and the possibility of endless reassembly offers creative adventure with none of the old craft skills and taboos. Paper clay has endless potential and is open to development, new methods and ideas appearing almost regularly. Maybe you can add something to this exciting area?

8

Glaze

WHYS AND WHEREFORES

Clay, changed by heat into a new, ceramic material, is hard, permanent and porous. Utilitarian functions are limited, however, as liquids will be absorbed into the body, eventually seeping out. Liquid remaining within the biscuit body will soon discolour the vessel and, more important, turn rancid. In short, the object is unhygienic and potentially dangerous. Porous bodies therefore need to be sealed to prevent incursions of liquids. The porosity of a biscuit-fired cup would make it a most unpleasant drinking vessel too – imagine the disgusting sucking sensation that would be caused by putting moist lips to a porous mug! From a purely practical point of view then, glaze could be regarded as essential.

The warm colouring of unglazed terracotta plant pots is certainly quite agreeable, but grey clay bodies lack even this limited attribute. In addition to their drawbacks in functional terms as mentioned above, pieces made from grey clays are also usually aesthetically unappealing. Glazes applied to such pots thus have a cosmetic purpose; they enhance and beautify ware which otherwise would be drab and boring. Such wares would discolour very quickly in use and become even more unattractive, particularly if associated with food and drink.

As a general rule, wares intended for domestic use at least must resist absorption. Most people are at least unconsciously aware of glaze, and recognize the need for it when actually confronted with the question. It is quite surprising, however, that many students at the beginner level imagine that some sort of paint or varnish provides this protective, cosmetic coat. Imagine what would happen if such a coating was applied to a mug containing hot tea or a casserole subjected to the rigours of a domestic oven! It can therefore be seen that such a solution would really not do. Any covering to the clay should be similarly 'ceramic' in that it has a similar response to heat, and it should be at least as durable as the vessel to which it is applied.

What is Glaze?

To understand glaze it is first necessary to know what it is. A student's second contact with glaze, the first being the thousands of glazed pots experienced in everyday life, is a bucket of runny stuff in a pottery workshop. It is often white or off-white in colour, sometimes will be a pale red-brown and sometimes it will be grey. It will have a label proclaiming it to be 'Speckled Oatmeal', Tenmoku or Lavender Blue, but it will look nothing like this at all!

Like clays, glaze mixes change colour and character after being subjected to great heat, so do not be guided by the unfired appearance of the contents of the bucket. Apart from a label, glaze buckets should be identified clearly by some sort of sample tile, firmly attached to the bucket rather than the lid. This sample will indicate the fired consequence of applying the contents of its parent container to subsequent pieces. Few if any clues as to what the glaze will look like when fired can be gleaned from the visual appearance of a glaze mix; neither does it indicate what the mix contains.

Perceptive students soon make the connection between glaze, glazing and glass. Based on the schoolboy notion that glass is simply melted sand, it could be, and frequently is assumed that the bucket will contain finely ground sand and that the heat in the firing process will transform this into a glass. Such a simple explanation is very appealing but unfortunately it just will not do. If a hypothetical application of sand to ware, this then being subjected to heat, does not on its own produce a glaze, then is the desired process somehow in part chemical? Rather than becoming involved with the chemical theory of glaze, it might be useful to refer back to material that is inappropriate in ceramic terms – paint. The allegory will, however, offer clues as to what is required in developing glaze.

To work effectively, paint requires three basic ingredients: pigment for colour; vehicle, to transport the pigment; and adhesive, to ensure that the pigment stays in place. Finely ground sand mixed with water cannot be considered paint. As an intended coating, the mixture has only a pigment carried, in theory at least, by a vehicle. Even if the mixture could be held in suspension long enough for a coating to be applied to the porous body, there is nothing in the recipe to provide adhesion. The addition of some sort of glue would solve this latter problem and complete the triadic structure of paint, and so biscuit ware could in this way be covered with a coating of sand prior to its placement in a kiln.

The first drawback to this solution is that any glue which is animal- or vegetable-based will be burned away long before the sand has been converted to glass, even assuming that this is going to happen. Sand would simply drop off any non-horizontal surface to leave the ware exactly as it was prior to coating.

The second drawback concerns the nature of sand. Although this familiar and very common material will contain large proportions of silica, the basis of glass, it will also contain other materials. Sand is a mixture of material that has been broken down by weathering and ground down by mechanical erosion, so it is likely to contain other mineral content (such as ground-up shells) and vegetable matter in addition to the desired silica content. Such additional material will not be quantifiable, might or might not burn away during firing, and will inevitably have unpredictable effects upon outcomes. In spite of the fact that silica would, on its own, make an excellent glaze in theory, in practice it is too refractory, requiring a temperature of 1,713°C to melt. Such temperature is beyond the bounds of practicality on technical grounds and in simple economic terms.

These technical difficulties arise from the fact that clay bodies will melt at lower temperatures that are resisted by the highly refractory silica. Apart from the obvious consequences to overfired wares, just about everything else used in the firing process would be put at risk. Kiln furniture, to say nothing of kilns themselves, make use of ceramic materials which are highly refractory. Inevitably, these would start to break down or collapse well before the required 1,700°C is approached.

The economic drawbacks, meanwhile, can be illustrated as follows. The thermal energy required to boil a kettle is relatively modest, but an immersion heater that is kept on twenty-four hours a day will very soon clock up a disturbing bill, even when heating water to less than 100°C. As maximum temperature is increased, so too is the cost. Economically, it would be prohibitive for the craft potter, or industry for that matter, to attempt to melt unadulterated silica. Most of us consider the acceptable method expensive enough when achieving fluxing temperatures in the range 1,000–1,300°C.

The cost of purchasing pure silica is also a consideration. It is available to the potter in the form of quartz or flint, both of which will have been processed and packaged at the customer's expense. As flint is also very hazardous to health (*see* Appendix), its unnecessary use is not recommended in any event.

A safer and more cost-effective source of silica is to be found in a potter's basic material – clay. The theoretical formula for clay is:

$$\underset{\text{alumina}}{Al_2O_3} \quad \underset{\text{silica}}{2SiO_2} \quad \underset{\text{water}}{2H_2O}$$

Clay therefore clearly provides a natural source of silica. Alumina is also an important contributor to glaze, as will be seen below, and is more refractory than silica, melting at 2,050°C.

But what about the chemical composition of real, natural clays? The formulae of secondary clays, such as ball clays, vary significantly, and these therefore have different basic properties.

An average ball clay has the following composition:

$$Al_2O_3.4SiO_2.2H_2O.0\cdot1K_2O$$

Where the silica content is less, the clay will be said to be aluminous; if the silica content is higher, the clay is siliceous:

alumina	silica	water	potash (potassium oxide)	
Al_2O_3	$4SiO_2$	$2H_2O$	$0.1K_2O$	average
Al_2O_3	$2SiO_2$	$2H_2O$	$0.1K_2O$	aluminous
Al_2O_3	$9SiO_2$	$2H_2O$	$0.2K_2O$	siliceous

Table 1   Content of ball clays.

	China clay	Ball clay (blue)	Ball clay (Devon)	Ball clay (Hymod red) (Devon)	Ball clay (Dorset)	Ball clay (or sedimentary)
Alumina	38.3%	33.5%	25%	25%	29%	33.3%
Silica	46.6%	46.5%	70%	60%	55%	47.3%
Potassium oxide (K_2O)	–	–	–	–	–	1.7%
Sodium oxide (Na_2O)	–	–	–	–	–	0.2%
Calcium oxide (CaO)	–	–	–	–	–	0.2%
Magnesium oxide (MgO)	–	–	–	–	–	0.3%
Iron oxide (Fe_2O_3)	–	–	0.8%	2.5%	2.5%	1.0%
Note The table suggests typical percentage ingredients, but check supplier's data for specific information.						

Table 2   Typical ingredients in different ball clays.

As can be seen, these ball clays have the additional ingredient of potash, not present in China clay (formulated above as theoretical clay). Natural red clays may have collected other impurities in addition to the red iron oxide (Fe_2O_3) which imparts the characteristic terracotta colouring. Such oxides can cause the body to vitrify at lower temperatures than China clay, acting as fluxes on the parent body.

As we appear to be rushing headlong into chemistry and making use of terms so far undefined, perhaps a brief deviation is necessary here.

Vitrification
This is heating a clay body sufficiently to cause it to become malleable, or soft, and on the point of collapse. If subjected to pressure at this stage, a pot will sag unless supported by the strength of its form (*see also* Chapter 1).

This vitrification results from the fluxing of free silica and feldspathoids (*see* below) in the clay. On cooling, the mass is seen to have been welded together by a glassy matrix which gives rise to a virtually non-porous body, and is usually considered to be a characteristic of stoneware.

Flux
Ceramic fusion is promoted by an oxide interacting with other oxides. Alkaline oxides interact with the glass to form silica.

Feldspathoids
These are feldspathic minerals, the most common

being Cornish stone and nepheline syenite. Others include granite, petalite and spodumene (these will be discussed in a later section).

To recap, therefore, clay contains silica which cannot provide a glaze on its own, but probably can with additions of fluxes. These fluxes are also natural, mineral materials, almost as readily available as clay. Given this basis for experiment, perhaps a glaze can be developed?

Above we have identified silica (to provide a glass) and flux (to melt the silica); the spare ingredient is alumina. This coincidentally acts as an adhesive, binding the glaze to the ware and adding viscosity to prevent the glass running off when molten. So:

$$Glaze = silica + flux + adhesive$$

The silica comes from mineral sources (*see* Appendix), including clay, the flux melts the silica, and the adhesive (alumina) sticks the glaze to its ware. Glaze can be modified to suit a potter's individual requirements by adjusting relative amounts in a recipe.

TYPES OF GLAZE

Surface Texture

If a perfect balance of fluxes, alumina and silica is achieved, in theory we should have a smooth, shiny glass or glaze. The balance will alter depending on the intended firing temperature. Earthenware glazes, which melt at lower temperatures, require more flux and less alumina and silica than do stoneware and porcelain glazes.

A theoretical imbalance of materials will result in matt or semi-matt glazes. A matt glaze containing a surfeit of alumina is referred to as alumina matt, if silica is in excess, it is called silica matt, and where barium is predominant it is a barium matt. Where one oxide is predominant, or is even the only oxide present, matt glaze will often result. This is because certain fluxes act in reverse beyond a critical point, stopping the melt rather than precipitating it. As a general rule, the more fluxing oxides there are present, the better the glaze.

Surface Quality

Specific minerals will give a perfect, or near-perfect glaze, certain characteristics of which are likely to be very subtle. Such loose terms as 'thin', 'lardy' or 'waxy' might be used to describe the appearance of such a glaze. Borax used for earthenware glazes gives a brighter, glassier look than lead-based glazes; high-fired glazes that are rich in feldspar have a 'fatty' quality, do not usually run, and tend to obliterate sgraffitoed or impressed decoration.

Beware of shiny glazes with high calcium content (from whiting, for example) which have a tendency to run. Although they seem ideal for sgraffitoed pots, glaze can be channelled down cuts and encouraged to run off at the foot. Added, rubbed-in oxides and overfiring increase the possibility of this occurring – and of a ruined kiln shelf and damaged pot. On the other hand, these glazes often produce beautiful surfaces reflecting variations in thickness, fluidity and colour changes.

Magnesium, added to glaze in the form of magnesium carbonate or talc, usually gives rise to 'buttery', 'soft' or 'silky' surfaces, whereas dolomite glazes, however attractive, have surfaces pitted with pin-holes, these therefore tending to be unacceptable for domestic wares.

Glazes with an opalescent quality can be obtained by the use of bone ash, comprised of phosphorus and calcium. Minute bubbles suspended below the glaze surface reflect light, thereby giving rise to this effect. The presence of small quantities of iron oxide can cause the reflected light to appear blue, as in Chun glazes. Other sources of phosphorus are wood and other vegetable ash, these all giving glazes such opalescence.

Any colouring oxides present in a glaze mix will react with different fluxes in different ways, thereby giving rise to endless subtle changes in colour, texture and quality. These can be explored by testing and observation, using bought-in, refined ingredients. Locally won ingredients, lacking conformity and consistency, will offer exciting, if unpredictable possibilities and are well worth exploring. For example, a glaze using wood ash from a garden bonfire will almost certainly yield an unrepeatable combination of fluxes because next time it will contain a different combination of woods and vegetable stuffs.

Thickness of Glaze

Only experience can help in determining whether to apply a glaze thickly or thinly. In the same way, variations in temperature in different positions in the kiln will have to be checked in order to ascertain how variations in colour come about, or problems such as running or underfiring arise.

Underfiring and Overfiring

A theoretically perfect, shiny, transparent glaze will only be perfect when fired to its designated fusing temperature. If fired below that point the glaze will not have melted or fluxed sufficiently to produce a shiny glaze and will be matt and opaque. A glaze formulated to be matt at, say, 1,250°C may well flux to a shine at a higher temperature. So, in theory at least, a matt glaze can simply be underfired glaze. A glaze which turns to glass and runs could similarly be said to be overfired.

The firing cycle causes several changes to glaze, the precise order of which will vary from glaze to glaze. Part one of the metamorphosis takes place when the kiln has heated to a red/orange colour, probably in excess of 1,000°C. At this stage sintering takes place, where the glaze ingredients melt together loosely. As the heat increases there is interaction between the various ingredients and the glaze begins to boil. If this vigorous activity is ended by cooling, the glaze will eventually be seen to be pin-holed and probably matt, but if the kiln temperature is increased still further then the maturing temperature of the glaze will be reached. At this point, the surface settles down, filling over the pin-holes. Overfiring may cause the boiling to recommence, causing possible pitting or bloating of the surface, and very probably the glaze will run; its appearance and fit may well be adversely affected.

Firing Temperatures

As the foregoing will have suggested, glazes melt at specific temperatures. That is to say, they are designed to fit particular firing schedules and clay bodies, the critical variable in all this being temperature. Ingredients must therefore be selected to suit this variable and should be seen as dependent upon it.

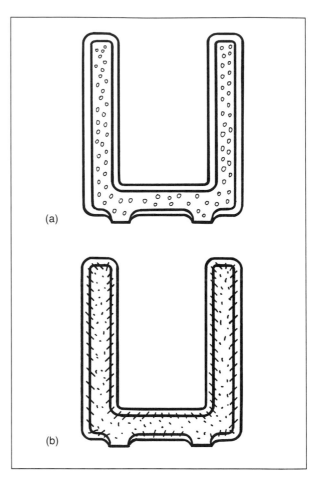

Fig 116 (a) earthenware – porous body with distinct additional layer of glaze; this can chip, craze or flake off.
(b) stoneware – vitrified body with glaze fused onto and welded into body; thermal shock resistant.

Firing ranges can be considered as falling into two basic categories:

- Low/medium; 850–1,100°C; earthenware/raku.
- High; 1,200–1,300°C+; stoneware/porcelain.

Earthenwares are porous bodies protected and enhanced by glazes; stoneware and porcelain have been subjected to temperatures which enable a further metamorphosis to take place, whereby the body of the ware vitrifies. This renders the piece impermeable, so that glaze is less functional and serves more of a cosmetic role. As the name suggests, earthenware tends to be softer and less durable than stoneware. The latter has virtually undergone an igneous reversal process, returning it to a condition similar in some respects to its material of origin via a subjection to intense heat.

I shall now sum all this up. A stoneware glaze intended for use at 1,250°C and giving a shiny, transparent surface, will be matt, white and porous when fired to a typical earthenware-glaze melt temperature of 1,100°C. Solution: refire to the correct temperature, possibly taking advantage of the sintered surface for additional decoration.

Earthenware glazes that have been overfired to stoneware temperatures cannot be saved. The glaze will probably have melted and run off, with boiling, blistering and bloating, even to the body. The ware may well have collapsed, at least in part, and red clays may have been transformed into a bubbly consistency. The appearance of wares fired in this way is further disadvantaged as they become firmly stuck to kiln shelves. Solution: where two transparent glazes are in use, one for stoneware, one for earthenware, ensure that both are adequately identified. Labels on buckets and lids will help. The addition of vegetable stain to one or the other can provide an obvious visual warning to the person packing the kiln: knowing that the red-stained glaze is earthenware, for example, should ring warning bells when placing stoneware in the kiln.

DEVELOPING YOUR OWN GLAZES

Unlocking the apparent secrets of glaze recipes is not as difficult as it might appear. As mentioned above, the basic ingredient can be clay, which provides both silica (the glass) and alumina (the glue). Some clays also provide small amounts of fluxes, as indicated in the final column of Table 2. More flux can be obtained from feldspars; these precursors of clay have the same origins, but have not yet lost such ingredients as potash, soda and calcium salts, these being splendid fluxes. This phenomenon suggests that if feldspars and clays originated from igneous or metamorphic rock, we might even produce a glaze from ground-up rock. The problem with this idea is that rocks such as granite are not easily finely ground.

It is recommended that would-be glaze experimenters visit a local monumental mason's yard rather than Dartmoor to obtain suitable materials for eventual blending and firing. The slurry and dust that result from cutting, grinding and polishing could provide a source of raw material which otherwise might be regarded as unwanted waste. Experimenting with samples of such materials can be very rewarding, both in terms of actual success and in appreciating the essence of the craft, steeped as it is, literally, in earthbound elements. Obviously, such a source cannot always be regarded as consistent and so, even with the extreme co-operation of the mason, samples might not always be pure or from a similar parent rock. Nevertheless, it is better to have had a beautiful glaze for your exclusive use rather than not, and the inability to repeat it exactly will lead on to the development of other, equally exciting glazes. The search for the ultimate glaze is, for some potters, almost more challenging than producing the ultimate form.

Assuming that the bought glaze route is not really for you, how then do you go about experimenting to develop your own glaze?

We saw earlier in this chapter that a glaze consists of:

$$glass + flux + adhesive$$

and that these ingredients are all available, naturally occurring in clays and feldspars. The other factor needed to produce a glaze is heat.

As in any experiment it is necessary to be methodical, varying only one factor at a time. To this end you might decide to experiment with a grey clay that is readily to hand, plus some feldspar which, like the clay, is on hand in reasonably reliable quantities, and which is also readily identifiable. As the table below illustrates, the composition of feldspars varies. Manufacturers go to considerable lengths to provide products that are relatively consistent, so provided you know the supplier and catalogue details you should usually be able to repeat your recipes if they are found to be suitable. As naturally occurring minerals, feldspars vary in composition so that each has different characteristics when used in the ceramic process. Referring to Table 3, orthoclast is used as a body flux, having a wide vitrification range. Albite is more suitable for low-temperature glazes, yields different colour

	Potash (K_2O)	Soda (Na_2O)	Alumina (Al_2O_3)	Silica (SiO_2)
Feldspar potash (orthoclast; $K_2O.Al_2O_3.6SiO_2$)	10.3%	2.5%	17.5%	68.2%
Feldspar potash	12%	2.92%	18.5%	65.8%
Feldspar soda (Albite; $Na_2O.Al_2O_3.6SiO_2$)	2.8%	8.5%	21.2%	66.4%
Nepheline syenites (typically $K_2O.2Na_2O.4Al_2O_3.8SiO_2$)	9.0%	7.0%	25%	56%

Table 3   Typical feldspars.

responses to potash feldspar, and is more vigorous. Nepheline syenites have a lower melting point than other feldspars, so these can replace others when lower maturing ranges are required. It is important to ensure that each feldspar is identified clearly with the supplier and catalogue reference number, or at least whether it is potash, soda or a mixture. All tests should similarly be clearly marked, coded and recorded to enable you to compare results and duplicate recipes.

The First Experiment

Independent variable
  Heat   1,250°C
Dependent variables
  Clay (earthenware or garden) ⎫ variable in
  Feldspar   ⎭ quantity

The ingredients (dependent variables) should be considered in terms of percentage/dry weight – in other words, 50 per cent clay, 50 per cent feldspar. Both must be in dry powder form. If the clay, for instance, is still plastic you will actually be adding 50 per cent clay plus water to the other ingredient and will not know exactly how much clay will be left when the water dries off.

If the above example (50 per cent clay, 50 per cent feldspar) is weighed out carefully, the quantities recorded and the ingredients blended with water into a single-cream consistency, this can be applied to test tiles or pots and fired up to the predetermined temperature (1,250°C in this

example) to check its fusibility. If the resulting test appears matt after firing, presumably the silica was in need of more flux; if the result is too runny a glass, there was perhaps too much flux for the amount of silica available.

Rather than wait for individual test results to appear from separate firings, which take considerable time even when using small test kilns, most potters use variations on the line-blend method, and fire a range of possibles in one firing. So, using the 50/50 mix as a starting point, it would be sensible to also weigh out a 60/40 mix of predominantly clay, and a 40/60 mix where feldspar outweighs the clay.

Clay	70	65	60	55	50	45	40	35	30
Feldspar	30	35	40	45	50	55	60	65	70

Table 4

Using the above table, it is possible to weigh out ingredients for a range of tests. Each sample needs to be made into single-cream consistency, and should be passed through an 80-mesh cup sieve prior to application to biscuit-ware test tiles. When sieving, make sure that any lumps are broken down and pass through the mesh. All weighed ingredients must end up in the slip if the test is to be useful.

Fig 117 Using a hog hair brush to push slip through a cup sieve.

Making Test Tiles

Step 1 Roll out a slab of clay.

Step 2 Cut out a rectangle approximately 4 × 10–12in (10 × 25–30cm).

Step 3 Cut the rectangle into 4 × 1in (10 × 2.5cm) rectangular tiles.

Step 4 When leather hard, bend each tile into an 'L' shape.

Step 5 Use a hole-cutter to make a hole at one end of each tile so that the sample can be strung up for reference, or attached to a glaze bucket.

Step 6 An impressed pattern will indicate how the test will respond to textured surfaces. Press in a screwhead or interesting plastic fitting if you have not made a suitable stamp.

Step 7 Biscuit-fire or once-fire. In the latter case, miss out the biscuit-firing and apply the glaze direct to the raw tile, preferably no later than the leather-hard stage.

Step 8 Dip the tile in glaze to cover the vertical part.

Step 9 Use a wash of manganese dioxide to paint

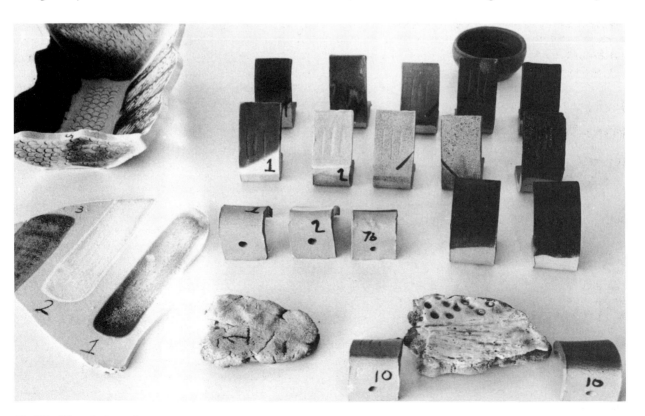

Fig 118 Glaze test results.

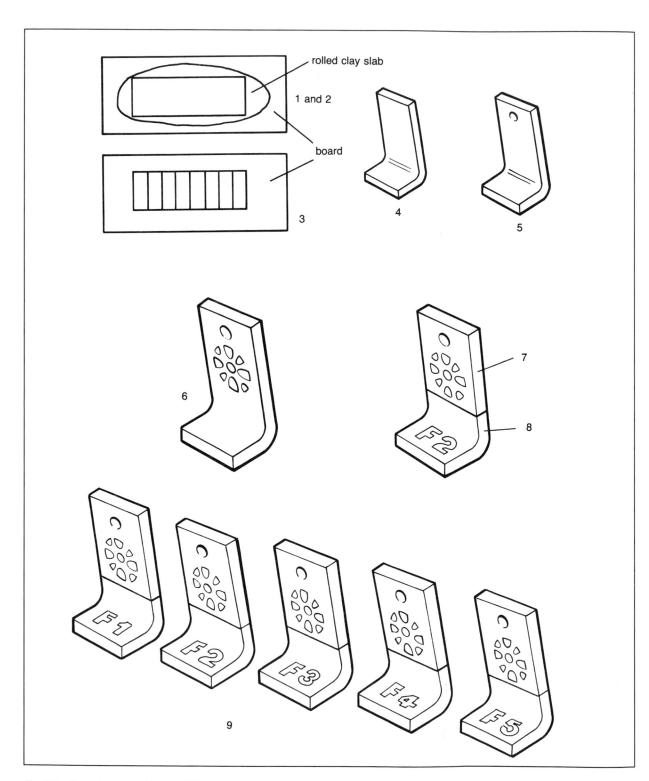

Fig 119   Test pieces, making and firing.

an identification code on the foot, where the glaze will not obliterate it.

Step 10 Glaze-fire; stand the tiles with glazed part vertical to check for excessive running (flat tiles will not indicate how a glaze reacts to vertical use).

I tend to weigh out small quantities of minerals on a simple digital kitchen scale which can record both ounces and grams. Chemical balances are obviously ideal for quantities of 3.5oz (100g) or less, but they tend to get dusty, cannot handle larger quantities and are rather slow to achieve their undoubted accuracy. Note also that extremely small quantities, however accurate, do not always translate into large quantities without changing fired characteristics. It is therefore sensible to test using reasonable sized batches. Even tests totalling 3.5oz (100g) sometimes fire differently than when used in working quantities. Having tested a 100g mix, I usually then mix a 100oz, or 6lb 4oz (2.8kg) batch and carry out the test again. If this test is acceptable it can then be used with reasonable confidence.

In the event of the larger batch not matching expectations, the recipe can be fine-tuned according to its shortcomings (for example, is it too 'fatty' or not fluxing enough?) using variations on the system outlined below. If you are testing ingredients which are easily and cheaply available, the best policy is always to test using larger quantities. And to avoid much tedious weighing, the following method might seem a reasonable alternative to the above.

Subsequent Experiments (Fig 120)
Step 1 Mix a double quantity of 50/50 mix (B).
Step 2 Weigh out standard quantities of 70/30 (A) and 30/70 (C) mixes.
Step 3 After applying mix B to test tiles, divide it into two equal parts and add one to mix A and one to mix C.

This will effectively give reasonably accurate 60/40 samples that require no weighing, assuming that the original test samples were all mixed to single-cream consistency.

If you succeeded in mixing exactly similar single-cream consistencies in the first experiment with 50/50 clay/feldspar, you will have noticed a difference

in volume. The clay mix will have taken rather more water to achieve the correct consistency – in fact, 3.5oz (100g) of clay will make up into about 5fl oz (150ml) of slip, whereas the same amount of feldspar will only make 3fl oz (100ml).

When using slip mixes in line blending, you must therefore remember that the dry weight ratios need to be built into your tests, so volumes will have to be divided into quantity not weight. If you have one or two graduated measuring vessels you should have no problem pouring off required amounts. Remember, though, that some slips will settle out more quickly than others, so always stir well prior to blending and when dipping test pieces.

The above experiment results in five tests; the first three are dry weighed and the latter two blended in slip form from the originals. Where more tests are required across the range, the sides-to-middle line-blend method is very useful.

Sides-to-Middle Blending
Step 1 Two blends, A and B (be careful to mix slips to the correct consistency, then divide by volume), are divided to produce C, which is an equal mix of A and B. For convenience, these can all be thought of as primaries.
Step 2 By combining two primaries such as A and C, again in equal amounts (taking care with amounts/volume), a secondary blend is made. Mixing the other combination of C and B will give a second secondary.
Step 3 The blending of a primary with a secondary produces a tertiary, four of which are possible.

The sides-to-middle system gives a test range of nine, which can be varied by the composition of the original A and B mixes. If you choose to test plain clay and feldspar samples as A and B mixes, five subsequent mixes will result. Using 80/20 or 70/30 clay/feldspar mixes as starting points, you will restrict the range more within the bounds of possibility. As has already been made clear, clay is not likely to become glass/glaze on its own, but testing the feldspar on its own might give some interesting results.

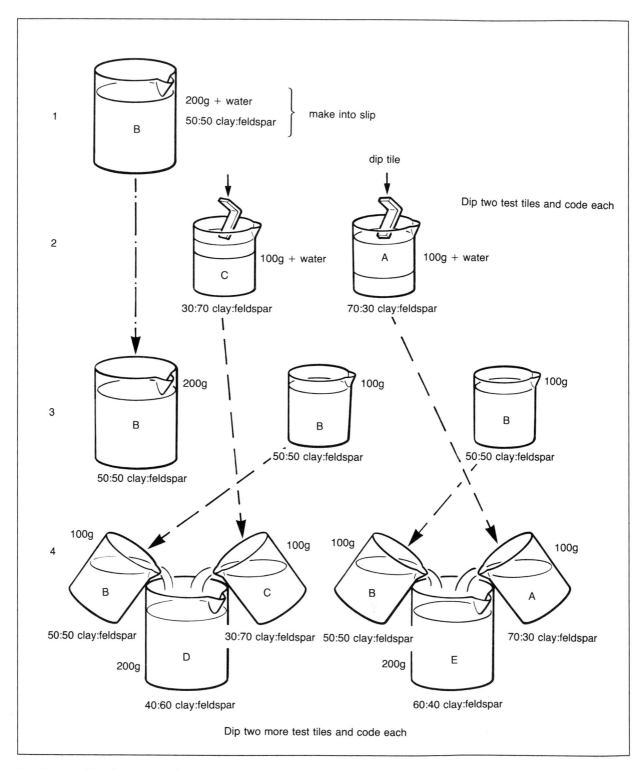

Fig 120 Line blends – dry weight.

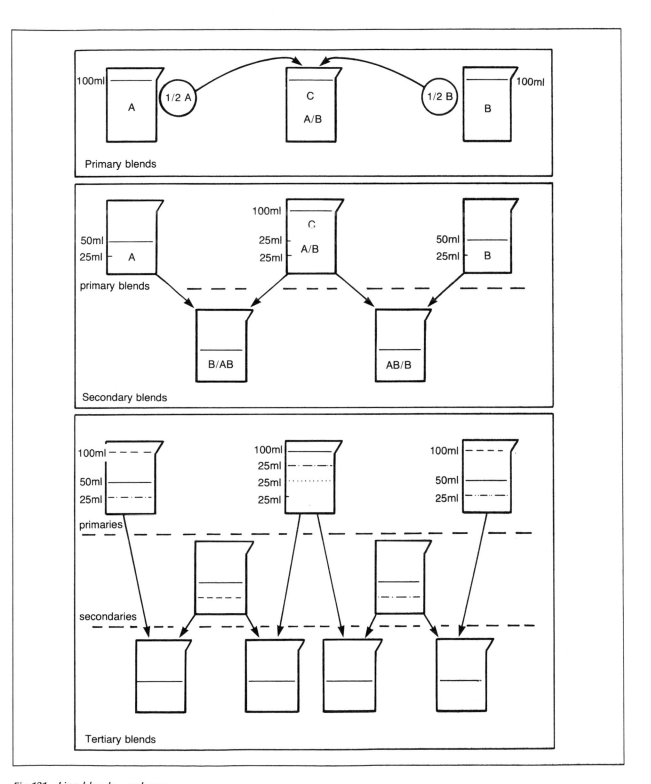

Fig 121   Line blends – volume.

C/F	C/F	C/F	C/F	C/F	C/F	C/F	C/F	C/F
80:20	72.5:27.5	65:35	57.5:42.5	50:50	42.5:57.5	35:65	27.5:72.5	20:80
70:30	65:35	60:40	55:45	50:50	45:55	40:60	35:65	30:70

Note Figures are based on a clay/feldspar order throughout – clay is given first in each ratio.

Table 5

The table above indicates the ratios arising from 80/20 and 70/30 starting points.

Calculating Your Own Tables
The above table illustrates the method for compiling a 70/30 table.

Recipes to Try
If fired test results suggest that a 45/55 clay/feldspar ratio is suitable as a glaze, all that is necessary is to use the figures as percentages – in other words, 45 per cent clay, 55 per cent feldspar. A working batch can then be weighed out as shown in Table 6.

If fired tests suggest that a mix between, say, 45/55 and 40/60 might be better than either existing test results, add together the two batches (carefully saved in anticipation of such an eventuality) and fire the mixture. Alternatively, re-calculate and weigh out 42.5/57.5 being the midway point (or average) between the two original test mixes.

TIP

When preparing DIY or bought-in dry glazes, assume that 10lb (4.5kg) of dry glaze will make a useful bucketful by adding 10pt (5.7 litres) of water. Initially, however, add only 7–8pt (4–4.5 litres), allow to soak (overnight if possible), then stir well by hand prior to sieving two or three times. If the mix is too stiff, add more water. Once water has been added and stirred into the glaze it cannot easily be removed, so be careful to add a little at a time until the required single-cream consistency is reached. To remove excess water the mix must be allowed to settle out (this could take several days) so that surface water can eventually be drained off, either by pouring or siphoning.

Ingredient	Percentage	Measure – dry weight	Volume – when mixed with water	Amount – av bucket
Clay **Feldspar**	45% 55%	45oz = 2lb 13oz 55oz = 3lb 7oz 100oz = 6lb 4oz	At least 6.75pt, where 1lb dry powder will require approx 1pt water	half a bucket or less
Clay **Feldspar**	45% 55%	450g 550g 1000g = approx 1 litre	Approx 2pt (1.1 litres)	less than quarter of a bucket
Clay **Feldspar**	45% 55%	4,500g 5,500g 10,000g = approx 10 litres	At least 20pt (11 litres)	more than one bucket

Note Amounts are very approximate and only intended as a rough indication of container size. It is hoped that the weight/volume figures will be helpful when using *any* recipe based on percentage amounts.

Table 6

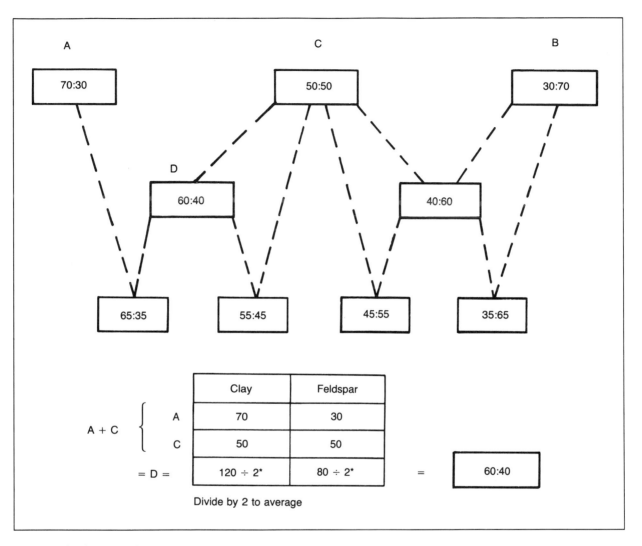

Fig 122 Blending model.

The Way Forward

So far, only two ingredients have been examined, and these only suitable for high-temperature glazes. This section looks at a range of other high-temperature glaze possibilities and gives suggestions for lower temperature testing, together with observations concerning health and safety.

Amazing discoveries and inventions have often been the consequence of pure accident or of doing something which seemed completely illogical but was found, after the event, to have been a stroke of genius. I have always been attracted to

the idea that simple glazes were discovered by accident. Imagine an early Chinese potter who, having placed clay vessels for hardening in a wood-fired kiln, stokes the fire with dry sticks. After many hours of careful, if tedious stroking, the temperature inside the kiln increases to an intense orange-red heat. The stoker, however, is mesmerized by magical visions within the fire; using a long stick to poke the ashes, he alters the scene and uses his imagination to transport himself elsewhere.

The poking action and the draught of the kiln, however, may transport ash up through the glowing pots so that some settles on their surfaces. The stoker returns from his reverie, decides that the required work has been done by the fire and so ceases stoking. After clamping up the kiln to slow down the cooling, the stoker retires to await the unpacking.

When eventually the kiln is opened, it is found that some pots (those that received a dousing with ash) have a glassy surface. Of course, it might then take a number of similarly spoiled firings to enable a connection to be made between the hot clay and the hot ashes, and maybe also the generally over-fired appearance of the contents of the kiln. The combination of clay, wood ash and high temperature would, however, soon become apparent, eventually leading someone to mix dry ash and dry clay into a slip.

This story is probably not far from the truth, for some of the most beautiful glazes used by early Chinese potters were simple blends of wood ash and clay, or limestone (whiting) and clay.

High-Temperature Glaze Suggestions

For stoneware and porcelain temperatures (1,250–1,300°C), it will be profitable to try the following pairs:

Clay/Feldspar (various – *see* Table 5)		
Clay/Wood ash (will vary from wood to wood)		
Clay/Limestone (whiting)		
Clay/Granite		
Clay/Basalt		
*Clay/Talc		
*Feldspar/Ash (wood or vegetable)		
Feldspar/Basalt		
Feldspar/Dolomite		
Feldspar/Granite		
*Feldspar/Whiting		
*Replace with basalt for further testing.		

Table 7

By adding several materials to the blend it is possible to increase the number of fluxes to a range of glaze tests. Such combinations of fluxes give rise to stronger melts than are likely with only one flux.

50 Clay 50 Feldspar	+	50 Basalt 50 Ash
50 Clay 50 Wood Ash	+	50 Feldspar 50 Granite
50 Clay 50 Limestone	+	50 Clay 50 Feldspar
50 Clay 50 Basalt	+	50 Clay 50 Feldspar

Table 8

The permutations are almost endless, but if a few two-ingredient tests have already been tried, some more complex combinations as suggested above will already seem more promising than others. For example, a simple test with a large quantity of flux and small amount of clay might seem too runny. By increasing the number of fluxes and still retaining a predominance of same, the first two couplings above seem likely to be more mobile than the following two at the same firing temperature. In any event, you are likely to get a good melt on one or more tiles along the line-blend test.

Low-Temperature Glaze Suggestions

My usual earthenware glost (glaze) firings are at 1,100°C, and I have had very positive results from the combinations in the table below.

Clay	+ Lead bisilicate
Clay	+ Lead sesquisilicate
1 part Clay + 3 parts flint	+ Lead bisilicate (4 parts)
4 parts Clay + 1 part flint	+ Lead sesquisilicate (5 parts)
Clay	+ Borax frit

Table 9

The firing range of any particular glaze can be increased by adding 5 per cent whiting to any of these blends. Try combinations using ball clays for transparent glazes and red earthenware bodies for honey/amber glazes.

Health and Lead

Lead has been used extensively in glazes over hundreds of years. It was originally introduced as galena or lead sulphide, these later superseded by white lead (lead carbonate), which was found to stay in suspension longer than the granular oxides and sulphides of lead due to its flaky structure. Deaths in the British pottery industry at the turn of this century ran at about 200 per year, due invariably to ingestion of small quantities of lead-bearing glaze over long periods of time. Both oxides and carbonates of lead are readily soluble in the stomach and can be taken into the bloodstream until their accumulation gives rise to symptoms of lead poisoning.

To overcome this problem, it is now customary to use lead only in fritted forms. By combining lead oxide with silica in specially constructed frit kilns, the pre-mixed ingredients are melted together to form lead silicate, lead bisilicate or lead sesquisilicate frits as listed in Table 11; these are not soluble in the gastric juices of the stomach. Together with good housekeeping practice, such as reducing dust, not eating and drinking in the workshop and wearing dustproof protective clothing, frits have minimized risk to the potter. Raw lead glazes are now outlawed in factories and schools in the UK, having been replaced by low-solubility glazes.

If, in spite of the foregoing, you are attracted to the undoubted beauty of raw lead glazes which make use of red and white lead and galena, remember that they are toxic. They can be used safely if handled with extreme care, and produce exciting visual results. For all practical purposes, however, the fired raw-lead glaze must be considered potentially poisonous. Such wares should never be in contact with food or drink, either of which can act like gastric juices to dissolve lead from the glaze.

Suggestions for Raku

Raku is mentioned elsewhere, but involves soft, low-fired glazes (less than 1,000°C) traditionally based on lead flux. The great British potter, Bernard Leach, suggested:

White lead	66
Quartz	30
China clay	4

Quartz is toxic as a dry ingredient and is therefore best avoided, as is white lead. So, start testing with:

Lead sesquisilicate	75
China clay	25

or try any soft-firing glaze or natural frit such as gerstley borate or calcium borate. Alkaline frits, borax frits and lead sesquisilicate frits will melt at temperatures below 1,000°C, and can be used on their own or in combination to provide a range of colour and surface possibilities. Hardness can be increased by adding small quantities of flint. Clay will stiffen the glaze in firing and act as a vehicle and adhesive prior to it. Used as an auxiliary flux, zinc oxide promotes an even melt, and the addition of 1–2 per cent bentonite and, literally, a few drops of calcium chloride will help to keep the glaze in suspension.

For further testing I will suggest only that usually about 75–80 per cent should be frit(s), the balance likely to be made up with clay, Cornish stone, flint, nepheline syenite (a soft, feldspar-like flux), tin oxide to whiten and opacify, bentonite and metal oxides to colour (see Chapter 6).

Glaze Ingredients

There are a number of very useful ceramic substances which can be identified as hazardous, but which cannot be avoided because there are no safe substitutes for them. It is therefore essential to maintain a commonsense approach to the matter. Risk from the occasional, careful contact with ceramics materials is probably less than those of other areas, such as photographic darkrooms or woodwork and metalwork shops. Adherence to good workshop and personal hygiene procedures will ensure that no ill effects are experienced, even by someone working therein throughout a working lifetime.

9

Firing

TRANSFORMATIONS

The metaphysical image of a ceramic holy trinity – earth, fire and water – is significant in several ways. First, it reminds us that clay requires drying and firing in order to be truly ceramic. It also conjures up an interesting idea of decomposed feldspathic rock being changed back to something akin to its original state; the process is reminiscent of volcanic heat, the centre of the earth, intense trauma and transformation, and of considerable risk. Finally, it can act as a reminder that materials falling outside the trinity are unlikely to be suitable for inclusion in the ceramic process, at least in the sense that they will not survive the metamorphic process.

There are three basic reasons for subjecting clay (earth) to ordeal by fire:

• To bring about a metamorphosis, or a change from clay into a unique and new material.
• To render the object made in clay safer and easier to handle as a consequence.
• To similarly change other ceramic raw ingredients into glazes.

In some circumstances, the final two processes can be achieved as a consequence of the first, although it is usual to progress in two firings so that wares are rendered safer to handle before glazing is considered. Reference will be made to a single-firing process later.

For industrial and studio potters alike, the firing process will normally involve two separate firings.

The First Firing

This is known as the biscuit-firing; clay is changed through a one-way transformation (metamorphosis) into a new, hardened, porous and rather lacklustre state. As its name implies, this ware has the appearance of biscuit, is not capable of holding liquids,

and so for practical and cosmetic reasons requires further attention. In some respects temperature is not critical at this stage.

The Second Firing

This is usually referred to as the glaze-firing or glost-firing. The prime objective of this firing is to melt or fuse a glaze mix on to the surface of the piece. In a glaze fire, top temperature is determined by the fluxing, or maturing temperature of the intended glaze.

Industrial and Studio Firings

The table opposite outlines the differences in firing temperatures used by studio potters and industry. The advantages to the industrial potter are in some measure offset by the craft potter's ability to create a system to suit a particular circumstance – for example, it is relatively easy to alter a glaze or firing schedule. And, because most studio pottery is, or can be, designed so as not to require complicated propping, the problem of distortion to plates is minimal, particularly as most studio potters will not usually be involved in producing long runs of bone china.

Properties of Fired Clay

Clay bodies react to heat in two ways, but to different extents and at different temperatures depending on their body type. Stoneware clays, which have a high maturing range, will need firing to temperatures of 1,250–1,300°C and are described as highly refractory. Earthenware clays, being less refractory, will mature in the range 1,100–1,150°C.

When fired to about 1,000°C, both types of clay will be porous. If firing temperatures are increased, this porosity is reduced so that at the maturing temperature the body begins to vitrify. Porosity

Firing	Studio	Industrial
Biscuit	900–1,050°C	1,100°C or more
Glaze	1,100°C	Approx 1,050°C
	Biscuit readily absorbs moisture – accepts glaze by dipping and pouring.	Harder biscuit requires precise consistency of glaze (applied by spraying). Use of binders or flocculents.
Advantages	• Easier. • More convenient for the studio potter.	• Tends to give better results. • Warping and distortion are likely to be apparent after first firing, avoiding problems when glazed. • Less chance of pin-holing during glaze-firing.
Disadvantages	• Body more reactive over 1,100°C in glaze-fire – escaping gases obliged to bubble some way through layer of melting glaze. • Distortions to glazed wares possible – cannot be supported at extremities, as in plates on a pin rack.	Hard biscuit/softer glaze allows horizontal forms – plates can be supported at extremities without risk of sagging.

Table 10

and vitrification both refer to the degree of water retention of the clay body after firing. This suggests a second metamorphosis: the change from porous to non-porous or vitreous ware, the latter state being virtually non-absorbent for all practical purposes.

To summarize, earthenware is relatively porous after glaze-firing, and so glaze is essential for cosmetic and practical purposes. Glaze is a separate layer over the body. Stoneware is highly refractory, its body vitrifying at temperatures similar to glaze maturity. It is non-porous, and so the glaze is mainly cosmetic and becomes integrated with the body with no clear demarcation line.

Correct Firing

A clay body can be considered to be correctly fired when its maximum degree of vitrification has been achieved without deformity, or when the body is capable of accepting glaze without problems of crazing due to imbalance in coefficients of contraction. The maturing ranges of clay bodies differ according to the nature of the body. Earthenware bodies, particularly terracotta, tend to vitrify early at about 1,150°C, eventually becoming rather bubbly in cross-section when overfired. Some stoneware bodies are safe, even in excess of 1,300°C.

In theory, any clay which has vitrified to its maximum, and has been glazed successfully (if that is desirable) could be described as stoneware. A highly refractory clay, fired below its vitrification point and glazed with an earthenware glaze matured to the correct temperature, could be described as earthenware.

In practice, however, deliberately vitrifying a red

earthenware body may overfire its glaze; this will affect the body colour, making it much darker. Applying and firing earthenware glazes to an underfired stoneware body (which then does not reach its maturing range) will cause problems with the glaze, and result in a friable body. Nevertheless, the latter practice is widely used in the raku process, more of which later.

SIMPLIFIED CHEMISTRY OF FIRING

Several very complicated chemical changes are brought about by the firing process, so that the firing must be scheduled so as not to hinder these reactions. From a practical point of view, however, these changes can be grouped into two stages. The first process is the formation of steam, while the second involves the combustion of organic material (carbons) contained within the clay.

Most water is driven off in the form of steam during the initial temperature rise through 100°C to 300°C. Carbonaceous material begins to burn away at 300°C, combustion continuing right up to about 1,100°C, and is released as carbon dioxide gas.

Silica – the Major Component

As indicated in an earlier section, silica (SiO_2) is a major ingredient of clay. The theoretical composition of pure clay is $Al_2O_3.2SiO_2.2H_2O$ or one molecule of alumina, plus two molecules of silica, plus two molecules of water, all combined chemically. Other sources of silica are crushed or finely ground quartz or sand, and calcined (burnt) flint; similarly refined silica abounds in volcanic rocks, feldspars and clays as a result of decomposition of rocks such as granites, and in sandstones.

Because silica is such an important component of clay bodies and glazes, potters are mainly concerned with the way it behaves when heated. Silica occurs in several different forms. When heated, some of it changes from one form to another and then reverts to the original form on subsequent cooling. Other modifications of the material result in a permanent change to a new form, which remains that way after cooling.

Two important silica modifications are of major concern to the potter: quartz and cristobalite. Let us look at the quartz first. Before being heated, quartz exists as alpha (α) quartz, but on heating it changes into a new form called beta (β) quartz, and expansion takes place. As it cools, beta quartz reverts to alpha quartz and contracts.

Table 11 looks in detail at what happens to the silica as it heats up. The higher the firing temperature, the more cristobalite is developed, which in turn increases the body's resistance to crazing. Underfiring a body, thereby restricting development of cristobalite, is probably the most common cause of glaze crazing. A natural earthenware body has a small expansion/contraction rate (approximately 0.7 per cent), while the expansion rate of cristobalite (3 per cent) is sudden, and is exactly reversible on cooling. If sufficient cristobalite is present in the body, the body will contract a little more than the glaze, which is thereby compressed and unable to craze. This cristobalite squeeze, as it is

	Event	Cause
Gradual expansion until approx 225°C	First sudden expansion	Cristobalite changes from alpha to beta form
Heating continues approx 573°C	Second sudden expansion	Quartz changes from alpha to beta form
Heat increases	Other forms convert to beta cristobalite	
1,200°C+	Most other forms converted to beta cristobalite	

Table 11

known, happens at about 225°C. It is invaluable in controlling crazing, but if overdone it results in shivering, the opposite and equally undesirable result of an ill-fitting glaze.

SILICA INVERSIONS

Sudden expansions and contractions at about 225°C, and again at about 573°C, occur each time a body is fired – in other words, during both biscuit- and glaze-firings. If firing or cooling is too rapid, the stresses set up by the inversions can cause dunting, or cracks right through the ware.

FIRING SCHEDULES

From the above, it will be seen that two sets of criteria have to be taken into account when considering the firing schedule. Regardless of whether it is a biscuit- or a glaze-firing, the steam/carbon factor will be present to a greater or lesser extent. Silica inversions and accompanying sudden expansion/contraction trauma may occur in any firing.

Biscuit-Firing Schedule

A safe and simple procedure is usually best. Identify the major objectives:

- Avoid excessive, premature heating as this would result in the traumatic production of steam and hence damage the piece.
- Oxidize as much carbonaceous material as possible in the first firing.
- Make the temperature (probably 1,000°C) safely, without mishap.

Follow the procedure below:

Step 1   A long, low, soak (overnight perhaps) to very gradually increase the temperature from cold to 150°C or so. The vent plug should be out during this period to allow free water to escape.

Step 2   If necessary, increase the heat input to build temperature gently over a maximum of two or three hours) to over 300°C. This will take it gently past the first inversion point.

Step 3   Increase the firing rate a little more to pass 700°C*. This will allow any lingering H_2O to be released without trouble, and will allow the second inversion point to be passed with a minimum risk of trauma. (Depending on the kiln, insert bungs, or close vents – probably at about 600°C.)

*   **Note** Beyond 700°C, full power can be applied to bring the temperature to the desired maximum; vents at this stage should be closed.

Kiln Variations

The time taken to complete the schedule depends to a considerable extent on the type of kiln in use. Older kilns were built using refractory bricks, which are usually dense, rather heavy and inclined to absorb heat. Because the bricks heat right through, heat loss is reduced by the use of thick kiln walls which then act rather like storage heaters. Much energy in the early stages goes into heating the bricks, so wares inside the kiln are consequently allowed to heat up slowly and gently, with an even temperature rise throughout the kiln. Due to heat loss at the upper end of the firing range, advances in temperature are similarly protracted. However, the disadvantages of time required to reach temperature and the cost of firing at the top end are offset by a natural schedule appropriate to the wares – in other words, the slow build-up at the early stages allows plenty of time for water to be driven off, inversion points to be passed safely and carbon oxidization to take place. Cooling down also takes time, again avoiding stress and shock to the wares.

Modern, hi-tech kilns make use of refractory insulation bricks, which, because of their open, porous nature, are much more efficient insulators. When the inside face of the brick is heated, the air pockets within the brick ensure that heat loss is kept to a minimum, air being a very poor conductor of heat. The outer face of the brick therefore remains relatively cool.

Other very efficient insulators used in kiln construction are ceramic blanket and ceramic paper, both basically made from ceramic fibre. This amazing product has become an important component in low thermal mass kilns due to its refractoriness, extremely light weight and incredible insulation properties. As a consequence, modern kilns are lighter, use less energy to achieve their tempera-

Stages	Temperature	Characteristics
Initial heating – water smoking stage (0–150°C)	0–150°C	• Free or mechanically held water is driven off in the form of steam. Replacement of free water will return the clay to a plastic state; the chemical structure of the clay is unaltered by its removal. As water boils at 100°C, it is reasonable to assume that by 150°C this first stage will have been accomplished. • Surface water is easily driven off and first to go. • Moisture at the clay's centre will warm up more slowly and require an easy passage to the outside. • Similarly, clay is heated first on the outside – see below. • Application of glaze causes absorbent biscuit body to soak up water from the glaze mix.
Dehydration – first inversion (225°C)	150–600°C	This is the removal of chemically bound water. Once gone, such water cannot be returned to the body; it is now a new material. This process takes place from 150°C to 600°C, with most chemically combined water being released between 200°C and 460–600°C, although some traces still remain up to about 900°C.
Oxidization – combustion of carbons and second inversion (573°C)	400–1,100°C	Carbon will be burned out in this period. Basically, carbons combine with oxygen, escaping in the form of carbon dioxide. When oxidization is incomplete a black core will result, as can often be seen at the centre of old broken house bricks. Occasionally, blistering or crawling glazes result from small black holes formed on the surface of biscuit ware, arising again from insufficient oxidization.
Maturation/vitrification (900°C upwards)	900°C+	The period when fluxes in the clay body start to react with the clays, softening as the temperature increases until they virtually melt. Fired beyond this point, the body would almost certainly boil, giving off gases which give rise to bloating or blistering, and leaving the pot on the point of collapse. There are two causes for the subsequent bloating: carbons oxidizing at this late stage; and temperature rising too quickly or too far.

Table 12

tures, allow greater internal volume compared to external dimensions, and are quicker and more economical to fire.

Modern kilns do, however, have a down side. Their very efficiency can be a problem as temperature increases can be extremely rapid. This can put contents at risk during the early stages of water smoking and dehydration, it ignores critical inversion points, and it can reduce the period of carbon oxidization so severely as to leave excessive amounts that will affect glazes later. The major disadvantage, however, seems to be the rapid cooling down of such kilns. A kiln packed with short wares, requiring a number of shelves (refractory bats) and props, and having a very dense pack anyway, will probably be less prone to problems than an open kiln with virtually no storage heater potential and plenty of air space. The latter will cool very quickly, possibly causing problems to the wares, of which more later.

The good news is that accurate and very convenient systems of electronic control have been devised which complement the hi-tech nature of the low thermal mass kilns. These are usually programmed to provide schedules for biscuit, earthenware and stoneware glaze-firing while enabling individual programmes to be added, or the programme schedules to be changed temporarily as circumstance might dictate. They usually maximize on fuel input, resulting in extremely economical firing cycles. Some of these controllers even take note implicitly of the rapid cooling potential of the parent kiln by providing a firing down facility. At risk of offending some suppliers, it is worth noting that such a facility might actually be essential in some circumstances – something not usually mentioned in product descriptions. If you are thinking of buying a new kiln it is well worth visiting showrooms so that you can actually see the items, rather than relying on descriptions in catalogues. You will be able to check out the thickness of the insulation, enquire about appropriate control units, and check the usual weight and external measurements, rating and power supply required.

Glaze-Firing Schedule

Traditionally, so I have been told, this is the easy bit. All you need do is turn on the kiln at about one-half power to drive off any water absorbed in the glazing process and to allow the kiln to heat to somewhere just over 100°C; as water boils at that temperature, all is well once it is exceeded. You can then turn on full power and let it rip until maximum temperature is reached.

Kiln Variations

With some of the older refractory brick kilns, this method may well be sufficient. The nature of the kiln, with its tendency to absorb lots of precious energy, is probably slow enough to allow steam to escape safely. The slowly but steadily increasing temperature will proceed through the inversion points without threat, only to slow up via a progressively flattening heat curve until it has reached its absolute maximum. Carbon will have plenty of time to burn away, while the increase progresses slowly toward stoneware-maturing temperatures.

The reverse process can almost mirror the upward cycle, except for an initial relatively fast drop in temperature. There is likely to be another chance for carbon oxidization to take place as the kiln cools, and little risk to the wares at this time. The final drop from 300°C or so can seem an endless wait, however, and here there is a threat. In order to advance cooling enough to get pots out,

one might be tempted to crack the kiln door at about 300°C. This will often cause dunting as sudden cooling and contraction coincide with the inversion contraction encountered at 225°C. This is the most likely time for dunting to take place; it would be a rash person indeed who would open a kiln while it was still at 500–600°C, when in the region of the second silica inversion point. So, avoid temptation and allow the kiln to cool in its own good time.

My own low thermal mass electric kiln utilizes a combination of HTI (high thermal insulation) bricks and an outer layer of ceramic fibre protected by a reflective steel sheet as outer casing. It is capable of achieving high stoneware temperatures very quickly. By trial and error, I have found that an energy setting of about 25 per cent power will increase temperature slowly enough at first; an increase to about 45 per cent power will then speed up the process sufficiently so that the temperature exceeds 700°C over the next six hours or so. By setting the controller (this is not a microprocessor-type programmed unit) to 80 per cent power, the kiln will still reach 1,100°C in another couple of hours or so. For earthenware glaze-firing, I soak for thirty minutes at the maturing temperature of 1,100°C to give a toasted (slightly vitrified) look to red bodies. Where a slightly lighter, more traditional terracotta body is required, the temperature is confined to a maximum of 1,080°C, with a similar soak period.

The soak period allows final oxidization to take place when the quicker increase rate would otherwise cause problems (small bubbles, craters or pinholing) with the glaze. To simplify, gases have time to escape and the glaze time to melt over before cooling and stiffening occurs. This extra time enables more heat-work to be done, so the body and glaze will be more mature.

Cooling Down

When firing traditional kilns, whatever the type of fuel or design, the major concern will almost certainly have been to actually reach temperature. The preoccupation with temperature increase would have arisen partly from the need to stoke and therefore have sufficient fuel to hand, and partly from awareness of the vagaries of the kiln and weather. Once the magical temperature had been reached and the kiln clamped up by closing stoke holes, the potters were obliged to wait. If the heating process took a lot of time, so too would cooling down. Some older electric kilns of my acquaintance have taken longer to cool down than to heat up, but this cannot be said of the high-tech kilns we use today.

Contemporary technology, at least in some respects, leaves little margin for error. There is a fine line between what is efficient when used exactly to design and what is not if used even marginally outside its specifications. In this respect, some modern kilns tend to work only just within the range of tolerance of clays. The consequence is that, if the kiln is not tightly packed with wares, has little in the way of kiln bats and props to store up heat, or the weather is extremely cold at cooling time, it may cool down too quickly.

There is very little that can be done to avoid such rapid cooling. If the kiln room is a potential icebox, it could perhaps be better insulated or firings could be scheduled for mild weather only. Vent openings and spyholes can be closed securely to prevent heat loss or draughts, and doors or lids should be checked for tight fittings. A ceramic blanket laid over the top of a kiln during the firing and cooling will also help to reduce heat loss. In the case of top-loader kilns, it is helpful to add an extra shelf or bat above the wares to help contain heat; the loss of firing space is likely to be more than compensated for by having fewer dunts.

If a kiln is continually seen to cool too quickly, the only recourse is either to fire it down or rebuild it. Usually, the practical solution to this is to fit an electronic temperature control system. The modest cost will soon be recouped in the savings you will make on fuel and elements.

TYPES OF KILN

Front-loading Kilns

The front loader reflects its historic antecedents, conforms to a traditional concept and can be constructed to fire with virtually any type of fuel. This type of kiln tends to be very robust, logical in design (based on the fact that heat rises) and is convenient to use. Packing and unpacking involves a minimum of stooping, enabling wares to be placed safely. Bats or shelves can also be placed

Fig 123   Front-loading kiln.

with similar ease as the inside of the kiln is easily accessed and visible.

Top-Loading Kilns

The top-loading kiln does not share all the advantages inherent in the front loader. Some models are less robust, and packing and unpacking can be a chore, putting stress on the potter's back. Placing shelves is not always easy either, and lids sometimes threaten to fall on the packer, although in fairness it has to be said that such a thing has never happened to me. Many years ago a student did end up head-down inside one such kiln, after her feet had slipped away as she stooped to place a pot inside. Only a modicum of dignity was lost in the event, although it did highlight a problem.

Fig 124   Top-loading kiln.

A major advantage top-loading kilns have over their front-loading counterparts is that they tend to be cheaper. The reasons for this are not entirely clear as they do work efficiently. They can, however, be less than tough to look at, and they sometimes do seem somewhat meanly insulated, putting them in the marginal bracket when it comes to critical extremes. Controversially, it could be said that they are cheaper, not because of their basic format but because materials have sometimes been pared back to the minimum. Some versions on the market appear to be more substantial than others, and although my own top loader is one of the thinner sectioned models it is none the less reliable except in the coldest weather.

Choosing a Kiln

When looking to buy a kiln it is therefore sensible to check the manufacturers' specifications, examine a range of alternatives and, best of all, talk to owners of the models wherever possible. It can also be helpful to have a clear idea of how the kiln will be used, or rather what it will be used for. A kiln which is fine for biscuit and high-fired stoneware, but which cools rather quickly, may not cope with the more 'precious' tendencies of slip-decorated earthenware. A combination here of, possibly, vitreous slips, inadequate oxidization, excessively rapid cooling and insufficient glaze compression can lead to disappointing firings not encountered with other kilns.

Where cost is of prime concern, there are probably three practical ways forward, purchasing a new top loader being only the first of these. Second-hand kilns are usually offered in local newspapers and in craft publications such as *Ceramic Review* in the UK. These can be extremely good value, having been purchased perhaps by someone whose enthusiasm has waned or who has used it irregularly over the years, hence leaving it in virtually new condition. Such 'low-mileage' kilns will have originally been purchased at pre-inflation prices well below current costs. Taking depreciation into account as well, they are likely to be half-price deals at worst. Cost of transport is another factor to consider, and if you have access to a sturdy trailer and a few strong bodies you have the edge on the competition. This may be a cynical point, but kilns are difficult to move, and vendors do like to clear the space and put the cash in the bank.

Building a Kiln

Another cost-cutting alternative is to build your own kiln. This has several advantages. First, it will be built on site, so actually getting it there is not a problem. Second, the various materials and pieces of equipment can be purchased as work progresses – in fact, it may be possible to purchase second-hand or surplus HTI bricks, burners and the like around which to design the kiln. Finally, alternate sources of energy can be considered.

Building a kiln puts one in touch with the fundamentals of ceramics in a very real way. Firing it up for the first time is awesome, exciting and reward-ing – an experience not to be missed if at all possible. However, further reading is suggested before you start, there being insufficient space here to deal with the details of such a specialist project.

It is possible, nevertheless, to experience at least some of the anticipation and excitement of firing your own work without the need for expensive materials and equipment. The latter part of this chapter indicates methods which are possible in the smallest back garden and which cost very little; they tend to be at the primitive edge of the ceramic experience, but they are utilized by some of the leading ceramists to produce extremely sophisti-cated work. As someone once said, 'Jazz ain't *what* you play; it's the *way* you play it.'

Pit or Sawdust Firing

This process can, literally, be as simple as its name suggests:

Step 1　Dig a pit sufficiently large to hold the in-tended pot and with about 6in (15cm) excess depth.
Step 2　Cover the bottom of the pit with sawdust to a depth of about 4in (10cm).
Step 3　Place the piece on to the sawdust.
Step 4　Pack in more sawdust until the pot is covered to about 3in (7.5cm) over its top.
Step 5　Ball up some old newspaper, add some bits of kindling wood and ignite.
Step 6　Cover the pit with a metal sheet or old dustbin lid when the sawdust has caught fire pro-perly.
Step 7　Allow the fire to burn down as slowly as possible.
Step 8　When cool, remove the pot.

So what exactly happens here? The heat generated by such a fire is just capable of biscuit-firing clay. It also smokes the pot, causing arbitrary patches of unburnt carbon to discolour the body. If the fire is allowed to burn down too quickly, this reduction process, or smoking, will be ineffectual and thermal shock may cause dunting. Raw pots are more susceptible to the reduction than is biscuit-ware, although they are rather more at risk.

Having briefly outlined the idea then, we have to go back to the beginning. Pots, either pinched or coiled, are usually made in terracotta, and are then burnished to create a compacted, tight surface which tends not to burn away at biscuit tempera-tures. To produce this shiny chestnut appearance, the surface is pressed and polished using simple tools such as pebbles or the backs of spoons. This is best done when the clay has dried slightly beyond leather hard but is not yet completely dry. Because burnishing takes rather a long time it is probably sensible to keep the size of the pot reason-able – say, not much more than 12in (30cm) high. The larger the pot or the greater the area to be burnished, the more the vessel will dry out during the process; burnishing thereby becomes progres-sively more difficult, until some parts may have to remain rough. Thrown pots can be burnished more quickly if worked on immediately after turn-ing. As the pot revolves when still attached to the wheel-head, pressure can be applied via a suitably smooth tool.

After biscuit-firing, burnished pots can be polished to enhance the surface and to accentuate

Fig 125　Smoked pit-fired pot.

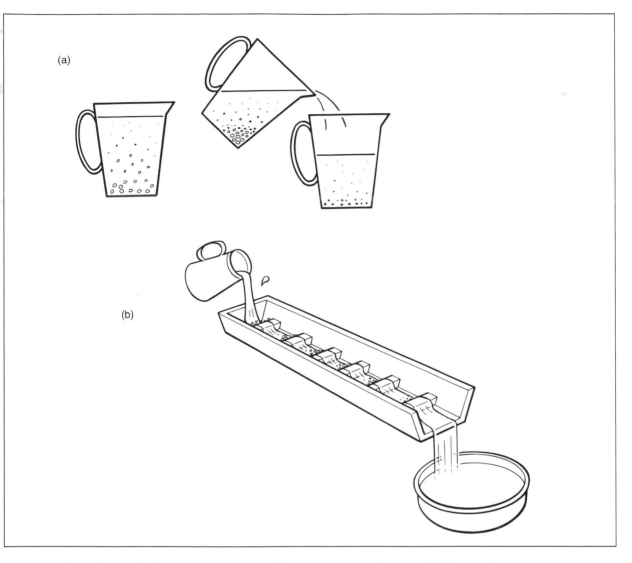

Fig 126   Refining slip: (a) by decanting several times allowing coarse particles to settle before each pouring. (b) levigation trough. Heavier particles settle out first; only the finest pigment is carried down into the final settling tank.

the warm appearance of smooth wood. The surface colour can also be enhanced by applying fine slips prior to burnishing. This will provide a superfine layer over an otherwise open body. Colour traditionally comes from the use of haematite or iron ore, which is almost pure ferric oxide (Fe_2O_3). This can be mixed into a creamy slip and applied to the pot, or can be deposited on the surface by actual burnishing with a smooth lump of the ore, as was once the practice in Iran and India.

The smooth, red, gloss finish of *terra sigillata* is achieved by using an incredibly fine slip refined by numerous levigations. In other words, after lawning, a thin slurry of slip is left so that coarser, heavy particles settle out. The slurry is then decanted, leaving the sediment behind. This process is repeated until only the finest particles remain.

After biscuit-firing, such pots can be polished to enhance the surface quality and accentuate the wonderfully warm appearance of smooth wood.

To add an extra dimension to the process, the unpolished pot can be reduced in a sawdust fire as mentioned above. The resulting black and grey gun-metal effects can be quite stunning. Where results are not to your liking, the pot can simply be reoxidized in another biscuit-firing.

Sawdust Reduction Firing

Rather than dig a pit, any raised container can be used instead. As the basic idea is to create a smoky, reduction atmosphere in the kiln, only a minimum of oxygen (air) is allowed in. An old metal bin or brick box will suffice. Some sort of lid will be necessary to act like a damper restricting the supply of oxygen, as will be a pair of protective leather gauntlets, worn when removing the lid by hand.

Old house bricks can be used to build the walls of the kiln; as this will only be a temporary structure, it will not require mortar. Just fit the bricks together closely enough to exclude excess air, bonding in as shown in the diagram. Using twelve bricks to each course and building five courses high, a total of sixty bricks will be required. If a square of chicken wire is readily to hand, lay it in the kiln to form a vented floor one course above ground level. This is not absolutely necessary, but it ensures an adequate layer of fuel below the wares.

Pack the wares in the kiln, allowing room for plenty of sawdust. Fine sawdust will burn more slowly than wood chippings or shavings, but both will require regular topping up to prevent premature completion – and more so if shavings are used. Once lit, the lid can remain in place, totally closed or slightly open as firing requires, except when adding more fuel. As a general rule, the slower the fire burns the better will be the results.

Some potters achieve a similar reduction firing within a conventional kiln using lidded saggers.

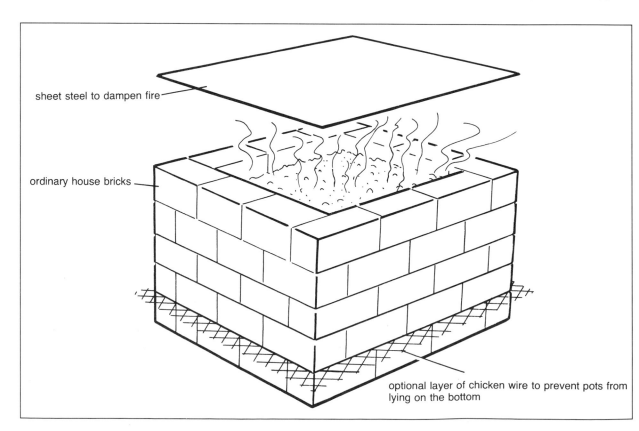

sheet steel to dampen fire

ordinary house bricks

optional layer of chicken wire to prevent pots from lying on the bottom

Fig 127 Sawdust kiln. Pockets of reduction and oxidization cause interesting arbitrary black patches to appear on the wares.

Fig 128   Allow ware to be in partial contact to prevent damage when settling as the fuel is consumed.

The pot intended for smoking is packed in sawdust contained inside the sagger. John Leach's 'Black Mood' pots are fired in this way in his wood-fired kiln.

Reduction in Electric Kilns

Current advice is that reduction should not be attempted in an electric kiln, but the occasional introduction of one or two saggars into a firing will not cause significant premature deterioration to the elements. In fact, another view suggests that occasional reduction firing in an electric kiln does not necessarily threaten instant death to the elements. Provided that the greyish layer of protective oxide built up on elements fired over a temperature of 1,150°C is not significantly reduced, no serious deterioration should take place. Two or three successive reduction firings will probably be necessary to remove the protective layer, whereas

an oxidizing firing will restore the coating to its usual thickness. It would seem sensible practice therefore to allow two or three normal oxidizing firings between reduction firings.

Whether a reduction atmosphere is detrimental to kiln elements or not, it is not actually terribly easy to achieve and maintain these conditions in an electric kiln. Many years ago, along with other enthusiastic exponents of reduction firing, I attempted to introduce carbon into electric kilns in the form of mothballs. Suffice it to say that a huge quantity was required, plus more patience than most of us possessed, and anyway it gave rise to the production of horribly noxious and toxic fumes. Naturally, we gave up.

More successful methods include drip-feeding oil or inserting a gas burner into the kiln. The best time to attempt such reduction is when top temperature is reached, continuing to add carbon, possibly in the form of charcoal, until the kiln has cooled to about 750°C. This excess fuel can be fed in via a spyhole or vent, but it is essential that the bungs or plugs are replaced as soon as possible to prevent an incursion of air re-oxidizing the atmosphere. It is necessary to stoke in this way every fifteen or twenty minutes to maintain reduction.

Summary

Reduction occurs when insufficient oxygen is available for the kiln to burn clearly – in other words, there is too much fuel and too little air. The result is often a slowing down of the heating process, and a chemical reaction whereby the fire burns oxygen that is bonded within metal oxides, particularly at high temperatures – for example, Fe_2O_3 (ferric oxide) is reduced to FeO (ferrous oxide).

RAKU – AN INTRODUCTION

Raku originated in Japan during the 16th century. Its recent popularity in the West is due to its process of rapid firing, plus the removal of ware from the kiln while red hot, the spontaneity and drama of the technique, and the direct contact with the ceramic process. Recently, the added drama of almost instant reduction has been developed in the West, thereby contributing exciting colour, texture and metallic lustres to the process. Raku has the additional merit of being relatively instant, in that wares can be glazed, decorated, fired, reduced and completed all within a single day.

My introduction to raku was through building and firing a wood-fired raku kiln with students. Our principle aims were to experience at first hand the challenge of achieving glaze temperatures using natural fuel, and to obtain a better understanding of kiln construction. It turned into a revelation to us all as we witnessed the melting and boiling of glaze – something not usually visible as it takes place inside a closed kiln and is beyond our control in a very real sense. Another valuable outcome was that the group developed a system of dealing with the various stages involved, almost without thinking. Co-ordination of stoking, placing and drawing out pots, and submerging the pots first in combustible material to obtain the reduction, then removing them and plunging them into cold water prior to cleaning, generated a group dynamic and

experience which was unique and essential to the success of the project.

The results of this introduction to raku were visually exciting: the contrast of the blackened body to the lustred and reduced glazes was in marked contrast to the subdued results of a typical stoneware firing. On the other hand, there were inevitable casualties due to the several traumatic processes involved, and although the decorative qualities could instantly be appreciated they soon became somewhat laboured. The completed items were also, in conventional ceramic terms, non-functional, so the very considerable effort involved in the raku process seemed somewhat inconsistent with the outcomes.

Over the years, raku has been developed by numerous practioners into a rather more refined art. Decorative techniques have become more sophisticated, with individual potters evolving novel and ingenious methods of controlling reduction, lustring and firing.

The Basic Process

Pieces for raku can be made by any process or combination of processes. They need biscuit-firing before being submitted to the extraordinary processes typical of raku. The usual procedure is as follows:

Step 1 Glaze and decorate the biscuit ware, and allow it to dry thoroughly.
Step 2 Preheat the raku kiln.
Step 3 Preheat the pieces to beyond hand-hot, to drive off moisture and reduce (a little) the thermal shock.
Step 4 When red heat is reached inside the raku kiln, carefully place the ware inside and close up the kiln to prevent heat loss.
Step 5 When the pot glows red and the glaze turns viscous and begins to boil, remove the piece using tongs. (This usually takes between ten and twenty minutes.)
Step 6 Immediately, lower the ware into a metal bin containing combustible material such as dry leaves, sawdust or chippings, and cover. This is the reduction stage and takes twenty minutes.
Step 7 Remove the piece with tongs or fireproof gloves and plunge it into water. This prevents re-oxidization by instantly cooling the piece.

Step 8 When cool enough, the piece can be removed and carbon deposits carefully scrubbed off under a tap.

Making a Start

The Clay Body

Special raku bodies can be purchased already blended to suit the process. They are usually very plastic but open, making use of grogs to assist resistance to the thermal shock that arises from imposed rapid heating and cooling. In fact, any clay that can withstand the shock will suffice. Much depends on how you use the clay (what will be your method of production?), whether there are extreme differences in thickness, and whether you work on a large or small scale.

Your first attempts could be experiments with various bodies – including fine, coarse, coloured and white clays – to see what might best suit your requirements. Bearing in mind what has already been said about clay bodies, it is worth repeating that some clays mature at lower temperatures than others. Predominantly stoneware bodies can be given a higher biscuit-firing to about 1,050°C; some red earthenware bodies will have similar porosity at only 850°C or so, given their much lower maturing or vitrifying temperature. The more mature a body is, the less it will be affected by carbon, thereby reducing possible black areas to greys. Burnished surfaces are diminished by high firing. You are thus free to select the qualities you consider most appropriate to your own work.

The Form of the Piece

Your piece need have no constrictions, provided only that you take note of thickness and practical considerations. Not only are there inherent dangers to the piece from thermal shock, but there are also physical ones – fragile appendages which survive firing can still fall victim to imprudent handling. A student scrubbing a wonderful teapot recently, and holding it by its handle, saw it shatter on impact with the sink. Such handling had caused it to part from its not immensely functional handle, even though ironically it had survived all preceding traumas. In the spirit of raku, however, the piece was reassembled later using an epoxy resin glue, and remains as aesthetically pleasing as it was before the accident.

Raku Kilns

These have become in vogue. A popular design on the market is the propane-gas-fired top loader, although numerous alternative DIY designs exist, again usually making use of convenient propane gas as a fuel. But is a special kiln necessary? In short, it is not. Glazes can be brought up to fluxing point in any kiln, provided only that subsequent steps can be carried out conveniently. The crucial word here is 'conveniently'. A raku fanatic I knew in the USA used to use an electric top-loading kiln. In fact, it was a largish model, standing almost chest-high when open, with the inner floor at just above ankle level. Removing pieces from the bottom of this kiln was not just inconvenient, it was downright dangerous.

Other inconveniences can bear listing: some top loaders are not fitted with lid-operated isolation switches; groping inside a kiln with live elements using steel tongs is certainly not good health and safety practice, and neither is attempting to look down inside such a kiln when tremendous heat is surging up into one's face. Sudden incursions of cold air do not prolong the life of kiln linings either, but that's only money.

Returning to the American raku fanatic briefly, his kiln, in common with most kilns installed in institutions, was located indoors. The reduction bins (sawdust, conflagration, smoke) were therefore indoors too – not to be recommended. So by this route, the answer to the question as to whether special kilns are necessary is, in practice, yes. Any raku or similar process requires adequate ventilation, preferably located outdoors, and preferably should be totally unconnected to electrical power supplies. Propane is a safe and convenient fuel, and raku kiln designs can be simple, and their use convenient.

Building a Raku Kiln

The major disadvantage with any top-loading kiln used for raku is heat loss. In order to place or withdraw wares it is obviously necessary to remove the lid, but by so doing most of the heat will be released, prolonging the firing time and increasing fuel costs. Even with a smoothly operating team working closely together, there will inevitably be a significant loss of heat each time the lid is lifted and pieces inserted or extracted. One answer is to

Fig 129   A simple 'drum' or top-hat kiln.

Fig 130   Interior of top-hat kiln.

Fig 131   Wares placed inside the kiln.

use a bottom loader, more commonly referred to as a top-hat kiln. As its name implies, this kiln is raised from its floor or base, thereby affording access directly while retaining valuable heat up inside the 'hat'. Pots can be placed on the bottom, or floor, of the kiln, and the entire structure lowered into place. This enables firing to continue with minimum loss of time and heat.

The oil-drum kiln I constructed consists of half an oil drum, lined with ceramic fibre, sitting on a kiln bat or brick base. A hole about 3–4in (7.5–10cm) in diameter was cut in the centre of the tip to provide an exit vent or flue, and the body was drilled at intervals to allow the ceramic-fibre blanket to be wired into place – sewn to the walls, the wire 'thread' protected from heat by ceramic 'buttons', which also prevented the wire cutting through the blanket. Handles were attached so that the lid

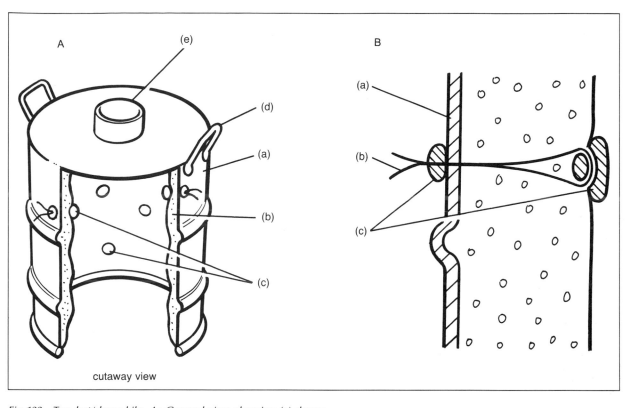

cutaway view

Fig 132   Top-hat/drum kiln. A: General view showing (a) drum;
(b) insulating ceramic fibre wired into place; (c) ceramic buttons;
(d) handles; (e) length of pipe. B: Detail showing fastening ceramic fibre.
(a) metal drum; (b) element wire; (c) ceramic buttons.

could easily be lifted using gloves, or a long shaft could be inserted through them to make the work even easier.

Simple Front Loader

For your first sortie into the exciting world of self-built kilns, you may feel that the above is rather too daunting, or it may simply be the case that cutting up an old oil drum is beyond the scope of tools available to you. A simple and effective alternative is to assemble a small brick kiln. This will only have a capacity of 1 cu ft (0.03 cu m) or a little less and will fire up with a normal gas-gun burner fuelled from a propane-gas cylinder. You will need about forty hot-face insulating bricks, offcuts of ceramic-fibre blanket, a few lengths of ¼in or ½in tubing and half a dozen or so old house bricks. The gas gun and cylinder more or less complete the list, but an old bench or table, suitable for use out-

doors, will make life even easier. The final capacity will depend on the size of bricks. The diagram overleaf indicates the basic construction of the kiln. Assembling it on a bench and base of bricks will bring it up to a more convenient working height.

Builders' merchants can often obtain HTI bricks for you; alternatively, you can contact specialist firms direct. Although HTIs are expensive and fragile, with careful handling they can be used over and over again. The bricks are unlikely to be adversely affected by raku firing, and even if broken they will usually fit together and work as effectively as ever. HTI bricks which are approximately 9 × 4 × 3in (22.5 × 10 × 7.5cm) can be stacked up into place one against the other without the need for mortar. The bricks are very easily cut or drilled as they are extremely soft, so a hacksaw blade and screwdriver (to drill through the bricks) are the

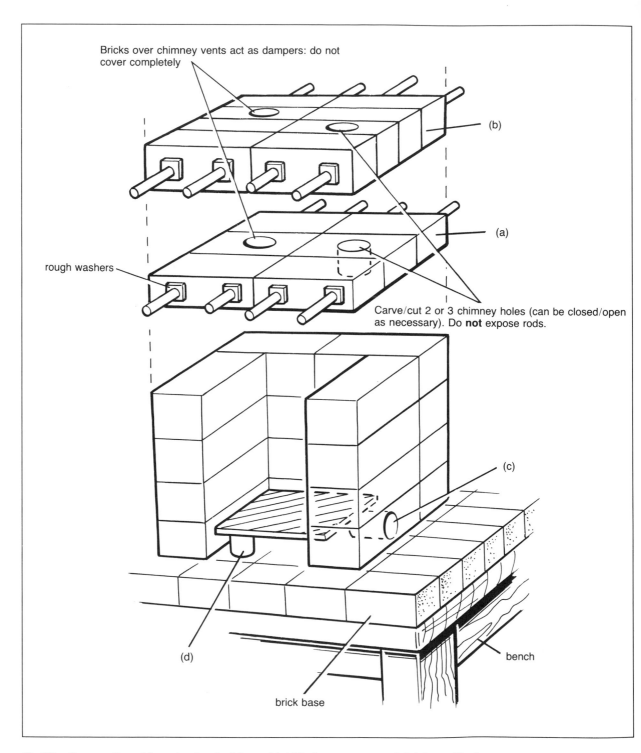

Bricks over chimney vents act as dampers: do not cover completely

(b)

(a)

rough washers

Carve/cut 2 or 3 chimney holes (can be closed/open as necessary). Do **not** expose rods.

(c)

(d)

bench

brick base

Fig 133 Construction of front-loader: build up with HTIs from a common brick base. The burner port (c) is either carved through or a gap (½ brick) can be left. Experiment with angle of burner/size, height of kiln shelf (d). Roof can be 3in (a) or 4½in (b) thick. Use mild steel rods to connect bricks.

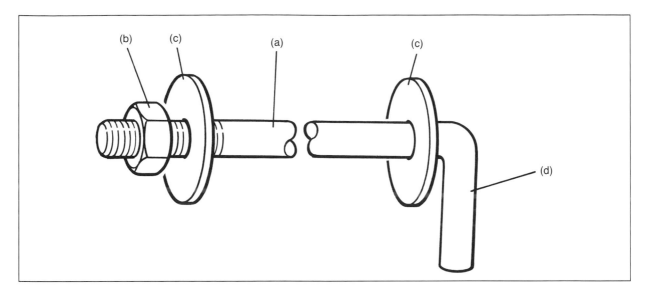

Fig 134   Rods with added compression: (a) threaded both ends or one end bent as (d). (b) retaining nut. (c) washers or plates to protect bricks.

only tools that might be necessary. The roof and door sections can be supported by internal rods or tubes. If sufficiently tight-fitting there is really no need for nuts and washers at each end, although the compression thus provided would give extra rigidity.

The internal chamber will be 9in (22.5cm) deep, 9in (22.5cm) wide and 12in (30cm) high, with 4½in (11cm) insulation through the walls. If there are sufficient bricks, ten can be used to form the roof,

Bricks required to build the basic box:		
Back and sides	16	HTI bricks
Front/Door	8	HTI bricks
Roof	10	HTI bricks
Subtotal	34	
Base (ideally)	10	HTI bricks (maximum)
TOTAL	44	

giving 4½in (11cm) insulation there also. A lid utilizing only six bricks laid horizontally and giving 3in (7.5cm) insulation will be sufficient, but a layer of fibre blanket laid over the top will ensure good heat retention where the bricks are not packed together tightly.

The bricks forming the front, or door of the kiln can simply be stacked up to close the kiln. If vertical stacks can be fastened to form two individually movable doors, access will be easier, but for maximum ease both stacks can be joined using horizontal supports.

Economy Version
A cheap version of the simple front-loader kiln can be made using any available refractory bricks, or humble house bricks. The latter will be liable to

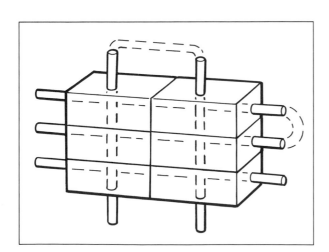

Fig 135   Kiln door. Either 3in or 4½in thick.

split apart from uneven and excessively quick heating, will take a long time to heat up in any case, and will form a much less efficient insulation. An inner facing of ceramic-fibre blanket could be added to overcome these problems, but as the bricks are likely to be cheaper than the fibre itself, their damage or loss will hardly be a problem.

The Actual Firing

With biscuit ware ready and a kiln and fuel to hand, it is only necessary to check that you have all you need to carry out the firing:

• A reduction chamber will be required. A large metal bucket, drum or old dustbin will be fine, depending on the size and quantity of the wares to be fired. A metal cover (dustbin lid) will also be necessary. This should be a third- or a half-filled with sawdust, dead leaves or virtually any combustible (waste) material. Ensure that you can understand and deduce the controlling factors giving rise to the effects you will have produced by keeping everything simple – in other words, intro-

Fig 136 (a–d) Fuming.

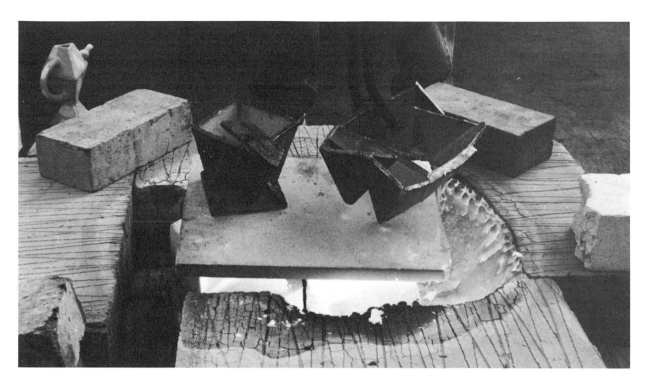

Firing: second stage.

Firing: third stage.

Firing: final stage.

duce only one factor at a time. So, see what effect is obtainable from sawdust alone before adding another combustible to the equation.
• Another bin/container with additional fuel is needed.
• A container with water is needed – metal for preference as plastic buckets have been known to melt.
• Leather gauntlets such as old gardening gloves should be kept handy.
• Metal raku or blacksmith's tongs will be used to handle pots when red hot. Long handles are essential.

Raku is essentially a group activity, so have two or three friends to assist in placing and drawing the pots, lifting lids, adding combustibles and so on. It also tends to get rather frenetic, so brief everyone about safety before you start. Ensure gloves are used when lifting lids, always ensure that propane-gas-supply pipes are well away from sources of heat, and warn anyone putting red-hot pots into the reduction chamber to keep clear of the conflagration as this can be quite dramatic.

Raku's universal appeal is due in part to the excitement of the process and the often unpredictable nature of results, but also to the fact that raku potters tend to evolve their own systems, equipment and preferences, becoming, as it were, their own experts. And so can you.

I have not covered glaze for raku here. Some suggested recipes are included in Chapter 8, or you may prefer to develop your own rather than purchase them ready made from a supplier.

Fig 137 Raku is essentially a group activity.

10

Personal Approaches

This chapter offers a glimpse into the working methods and thought processes of just a few contemporary ceramic artist-potters. In addition to the colour illustrations in this book, they have contributed insights into personal approaches that are often avant-garde and idiosyncratic. Traditional values and techniques are embraced, distended or extended to suit their own visions, these often broadening the boundaries of ceramic experience in some unique way. Their comments highlight and/or expand on ideas or themes suggested elsewhere in the text, and reflect the richness and breadth of the contemporary ceramic scene. Their accounts also reflect the fraternalistic generosity of a vast majority of potters, for they have been willing to share the products of their often very significant hard work, successes and frustrations, a great deal of which goes unseen.

JOHN CALVER

Carnforth, Lancashire.
I make decorated, functional stoneware. The bowl illustrated was thrown and, while still on the wheel, marked in the centre with a spiral. It was then squared off at its base and the rim altered. At leather-hard stage, the form was completed by turning the base, and handles and feet made from coils of clay were added. Decoration was also carried out at the leather-hard stage by trailing and sponging slips, sometimes over paper cut-outs to resist the slip. The surface was also impressed using stamps made from biscuit-fired clay. I also make use of fabric impressed in the surface of freshly thrown clay.

After biscuit-firing in an electric kiln, six glazes were poured on to the bowl in two layers. The first layer contained four partly overlapping glazes, and the second layer consisted of two partly overlapping glazes poured as soon as the first layer lost its

sheen. Working quickly helps the partly overlapping glazes in each layer to run together, thereby reducing hard edges.

Glaze-firing to 1,300°C, using oil as fuel, takes about fourteen hours. Reduction starts three hours into the firing at about 650°C and is continued until the end of the firing process.

JOHN DUNN

Open Studios, Brighton, Sussex.
I have always held raku to be sacred and have not been inclined to compromise in this area. My commitment to the production of raku dishes has consequently been single-minded and meaningful. The evolution and refinement of the large (23in, or 56cm, diameter) pieces I make has spread over nine years and more; I am now more or less convinced that, aesthetically and technically, I am left with no scope for improvement.

The dishes are made by pressing flattened coils into plaster moulds, starting at the centre and adding further flattened overlapping coils until the mould is filled. The coils are then flattened further and compressed to give a dense body that is resistant to thermal shock.

After trimming surplus clay from around the rim, a serrated metal kidney is used to start the smoothing process. The thumb is used to form the ridge and to profile the lip. Further smoothing of the surface follows using a metal kidney and, later, a rubber kidney. Final smoothing of the rim is effected with a chamois leather.

The dishes are biscuit-fired to 1,000°C and spray-glazed before pre-heating. They are then glaze-fired in a propane-gas kiln, using two burners which enable it to reach 1,000°C in twenty minutes. An unexpected feature of this kiln is the addition of a chimney, which, based on experience, gives best results if it has a height of at least one and a half times the kiln's diameter. The dishes, which are fired singly, are then removed from the kiln and laid into a ceramic-fibre tray to receive heat treatment.

Each dish is sprayed while hot with stannus chloride (which iridizes the glaze) and then transferred to a tray containing sawdust. It is covered quickly with aluminium foil to retain heat, a ceramic-fibre blanket placed over the top, and the whole wrapped up tight. Protective gloves are worn together with mask and goggles.

After thirty minutes the blanket and foil are removed to reveal the crackle and mother-of-pearl lustre effects characteristic of this process. The procedure is completed as the pots are washed with a scouring agent to remove wood tar and finally polished.

SARAH DUNSTAN

Potting Shed Studio, St Ives, Cornwall.
The porcelain slabs are decorated with coloured slips and textured before they are assembled. The shape of the bottle is determined by the width or length of this slab, and it is at this stage that the bottles acquire their own personality – short and fat or tall and skinny. With this personification, the other aesthetic considerations of legs, necks and handles follow.

Cracking is avoided in the finished bottle by careful drying over several days. After a biscuit-firing, the bottle is then glazed and fired in a small electric kiln to 1,280°C oxidation, and bottles then sometimes are re-fired in a 650°C lustre-firing.

I enjoy the play of opposites, with rough textures appearing against the delicacy of porcelain. I construct environments for the porcelain bottles in a frame or box made from a crank-like clay which is fired in a gas kiln with a dry 1,280°C reduction glaze.

VICTORIA AND MICHAEL EDEN

Hale, near Milnthorpe, Cumbria.
We have been working together since 1981, continuously exploring the possibilities of slip-decorated earthenware. Initially, our influences were contemporary and included stimuli from other arts and crafts areas. Over the last few years, however, we have been much more interested in tracing the history and traditions of slipware, taking our work much closer to what is the essence of the medium – liveliness, fluidity, rich natural colour and often humour.

A study trip to Hungary proved enlightening and started us developing coloured glazes, which we apply over a combed slip background. Such stimulation has given our work a great boost, and moved it a step further forward and closer to the ever-receding goal of the perfect pot.

We use a range of earthenware clays, decorated at leather-hard stage with various coloured slips, most being raw glazed and once-fired in an electric kiln. We also stain our clear glaze with oxides and apply these over a layer of clear glaze in order for them to run and melt together. We are just starting to wood-fire, hoping that this will add some incidental unplanned qualities to our work.

RICHARD GODFREY

Holbeton, near Plymouth, Devon.
Of all the forms and pots I make I probably enjoy teapots the most, largely because the sort of hand-built versions I produce involve a large element of three-dimensional doodling.

I spend quite a lot of time sketching and doodling, jotting down notes about ideas that I have had or things that I have seen in the country lanes on my way to work. I also pick up a lot of flotsam from the high-tide mark on the beach near my studio: bits of wood, plastic and metal that have been squashed, shaped and smoothed by the action of the sea.

The teapot illustrated was slab-built from five pieces of leather-hard clay. Once assembled, I allowed the basic form to dry slightly (for about two hours). This drying period is sufficient to compress the air inside a little, making the form easy to shape and smooth without collapsing. Once the basic form was complete, I made a small hole for the spout and blew gently, swelling the form slightly to give it more 'spring'. Now comes the bit I enjoy most – I start doodling with bits of extruded and modelled clay, squashing or bending them in any way I think might look or feel interesting. The handle on the illustrated teapot comes from a piece of bent pipe I found on the beach; it felt so nice when I picked it up I wanted to incorporate that element of tactile discovery. The squiggly bits on the sides of the lid that lock it in place come from the small, bright yellow shells found on most beaches.

The brightly coloured decoration was applied using a range of coloured engobes that I have developed over the last ten years. I brush, spray, sponge and trail these on to my pieces, and again the inspiration comes from the countryside and coastline around my studio.

FLORA HUGHES-STANTON

Nottingham, Nottinghamshire.
Contact with potters while on holiday in Peru prompted me to arrange an extended working visit. My previous work had been predominantly stoneware, having worked at Alderney Pottery in the Channel Islands. The South American connection was in stark contrast to the comparatively sophisticated procedures most of us enjoy in our European contact with ceramics.

Aylambo is a pottery school as well as a working pottery in the Andean mountains of Peru. The teachers and most of the students are from the indigenous Indian community, and after a period of four to six years at Aylambo most of the students start up their own family-run potteries. The pottery also acts as the local school for children from the surrounding area, thereby serving a useful role in the community.

Work produced at the pottery is made on the wheel or in moulds, and fired to 1,100°C. The clay used is found locally and is dug by the potters and students at the pottery. There are three main colours used for decorating: white and red from natural clays found near by; and black, from a local stone that is crushed and mixed with the white clay. These three colours are also mixed together to add further variety to the possible number of slips available. The stone and clays used are all crushed with a large rounded stone before being sieved and made into slip.

The colours are painted on to the leather-hard pot using paintbrushes made from old pens and donkey hair. Once the decoration is finished, a small glass bottle is rolled on the surface of the pot to press the slips firmly on, after which the bottle is rubbed over the surface to burnish the pot. For the bowl illustrated I used a lightbulb as it was more appropriate for burnishing the curved interior.

The pots are then wood-fired to 1,000°C. Pots that are not to be glazed are then polished using wax on the areas decorated with slip.

MELANIE HUNTER

Marlborough, Wiltshire.
My work carries a strong narrative theme, pertaining to the tradition of domestic ceramics. Connotations of still life, and of eating, drinking and feasting when captured in clay display a moment of time past. It is the spirit of that moment that is seized through the fluid treatment of the clay: the distorted coffee pot, or the stack of dishes. They describe the essence of domestic life, of things, and of piles and groups of pots through their relation to one another. Fragmentation, emphasis and flattening of the forms renders the pieces more conversant with a drawing or sketch of the objects creating a hybridization between the two- and three-dimensional images.

PETER ILSLEY

Whilton Locks Pottery, Daventry, Northamptonshire.
Dry copper raku I use a grogged body with good thermal-shock resistance, such as a craft crank or a mixture of commercial clays, ST-material and porcelain. The pots are thrown and biscuit-fired to 1,000°C, and either sprayed, brushed or dipped using a glaze consisting of 90 per cent black copper oxide and 10 per cent alkaline frit.

The pots are then raku-fired to 1,000°C, removed from the kiln and placed on a bed of sawdust sprinkled with white spirit. They are left to flame for approximately one minute before being covered with an inverted can, which is sealed around the bottom with sand and sawdust. When the can is cool enough to be handled, the pots are removed and allowed to cool; the colour intensifies as they do so. Pots that finish really dull can be re-fired.

Naked raku After making the pots – which can be thrown, slabbed or press-moulded – I burnish them with a polished pebble. They are then biscuit-fired to 1,000°C.

The pots are covered with a slip made of 60 per cent calcined China clay and 40 per cent ball clay. They then get a thin coat of glaze made of 90 per cent lead bisilicate and 10 per cent China clay.

The decoration is then carved through the glaze and slip. When dry, the pot is raku-fired to 900°C, removed from the kiln, placed on a bed of straw and newspaper, immediately covered and then allowed to cool before it is removed. The glaze and slip are then peeled off to reveal the clay body, which can be given a thin coat of beeswax.

Macro-crystalline glaze My pots are mainly thrown porcelain bottles and bowls which are once-fired (others may prefer to biscuit-fire). Porcelain is advisable because, apart from its whiteness and response to colour, it copes well with the glaze's caustic nature, which tends to leach material from the clay surface.

The glazes, which may be brushed or sprayed on, are based on the following recipe:

Ferro frit 3110	46
Flint	21
Zinc oxide	27
Titanium dioxide	7
Fine malachite	3
Calcined alumina	1

With bottle forms, the glaze is laid more heavily on the top and shoulder due to the fact that it is extremely fluid at peak temperature and may well run off the bottom of the pot. It is advisable to place the pot on a small posy, thrown at the same time. After firing, the dish is cut off with a tile-cutter and the base of the work is ground smooth. A typical firing schedule for the glaze given would be:

1 Fast up to peak (1,275°C).
2 Fast drop from peak to 1,090°C.
3 Four-hour soak.

WILL LEVI MARSHAL

Orchardton Pottery, Castle Douglas, Dumfries and Galloway.

Technical statement All my work is wheel-thrown. After throwing, I often alter the form in some way, usually by manipulating the clay at different stages in the drying process. I find that the clay responds differently almost hour by hour, and I try to be sensitive to these stages and exploit them. I believe this allows me a great variety of choices concerning the finished form.

Sometimes I like to draw with a soft pencil on to the dry pot to get a feel for the decoration. I have a second chance to draw on the pots when they are biscuited as the pencil burns off in the biscuit-firing. Before glazing begins, I mask out some areas with tape and adhesive-paper shapes. Small areas such as handles are painted with glaze and then covered with a wax emulsion; larger areas are poured or dipped. After waxing around the masked areas, the tape is removed. These areas are then painted in with a different coloured glaze.

After a glaze-firing of 1,280°C in an electric kiln, the pots are then selectively painted with lustre and enamel, and fired again to 750°C.

Artist's statement Broadly speaking, the choices I have made about material and process are derived from a personal need for reassurance and stability. This need is supported by the discipline of function, repetition and historical reference. Paradoxical to this is a need to take risks, be irrational and make mistakes. I am able to take bigger risks if the context is well defined.

The pots I make are often based on rational, functional forms contrasted with irrational, irregular additions and marks on the surface. I try to choose marks and colours that give structure and meaning to a pot. In this way I want to fuse a real object (a pot) with something which talks about reality but is an illusion (the realm of art), thereby fulfilling both the physical and spiritual needs of the user. A good pot should simultaneously confirm your coordinates and take you somewhere else.

I want to continue discovering and enjoying my work, and I hope others will enjoy my discoveries. To quote Robert Rauschenberg, 'Art is educating, provocative and enlightening even when first not understood. The very creative confusion stimulates curiosity and growth, leading to trust and tolerance. To share our intimate eccentricities proudly will bring us all closer.'

JOHN POLLEX

White Lane Gallery, Barbican, Plymouth, Devon.
My work is made with a buff earthenware clay, biscuit-fired to 1,050°C and glaze-fired to 1,120°C. Most of the work is thrown, and then the shapes are altered whilst the pots are still soft. This is done either by lifting the pot and then gently dropping it, or by striking it with pieces of wood. After the alterations have been made, the pot is further assembled by adding handles, spouts and the like. Once this has been accomplished, the pot is then covered with a black slip.

My ideas for decoration are mainly derived from the study of abstract paintings, my major influences being the works of Howard Hodgkin, Robert Natkin, Patrick Heron, Ben Nicholson and Hans Hofmann. First, I apply coloured slips with a variety of sponges, then I use brushes to bring a more painterly quality to the surface. I consider each pot as a painting regardless of scale, the object being to make each one different. The use of a transparent glaze completes the process.

CARLOS VAN REIGERSBERG-VERSLUYS

Vine Farm Pottery, Stamford, Lincolnshire.
I make my vessels using thrown and hand-built elements. The clay is incised, carved, impressed and torn whilst very soft using a variety of simple, hand-made tools. The vessels are then glazed using up to five layers of dry ash glazes. Accidents are exploited and often carry the work in a new direction; glazes are frequently cross-contaminated in the confusion of glazing and the outcome of each firing is awaited with a blend of anxiety and anticipation. My work is fired in a down-draught kiln in a heavily reduced firing to cone 10, an average firing taking twenty hours.

ANTONIA SALMON

Nether Edge, Sheffield, South Yorkshire.
'Unfolding' probably best describes the process I use to find new forms. I generally work on a series of pieces at any one time, the usual process being to sketch ideas, only some of which will be translated into clay. I spend many days stripping the form of each piece down to its essential elements, often with only a general sense of what is right or wrong for it. It is a lengthy process which I find difficult, yet it is also exciting and enriching because I am trying to be honest to the work and to myself.

My working methods are simple. I will use any technique I can master in order to make the work, from throwing, press-moulding and slab-building to coiling. I mostly use a fine white stoneware, introducing T-material for larger pieces so that they may better withstand the thermal shock during the sawdust firing. All the work is refined by scraping down the surfaces and it is then burnished two or three times using a spoon or a smooth piece of perspex. Although burnishing is practised primarily to create a smooth, shiny surface, I find that it is also part of the forming process in the way that it creates a cohesive outer layer.

The work is biscuit-fired to 1,060°C and then smoked in sawdust. I experiment with different types of wood and with packing. One of the attractive aspects of sawdust-firing is its unknown element, whereby it gives rise to the most exciting patterns.

RUTHANNE TUDBALL

Earley, Reading, Berkshire.
I throw quickly with soft clay on the wheel and with little or no turning of the finished piece. The history of the piece is recorded with meticulous fidelity by the soda vapour in the firing process. I aim to retain as much of the fluid quality of the material as possible and return to the user that tactile experience through handling.

My pots are manipulated while the clay is wet on the wheel. A teapot is made and fitted with a spout and a handle as soon as it is thrown, and is finished within about half an hour in order to capture the freshly made look of a piece just off the wheel.

In most cases decoration is carried out as the pot is thrown. I concentrate on methods of faceting (drawing on inspiration from tide patterns left in the sand) in order to exploit both the manufacturing process and the revelatory quality of a sodium-glazed surface that tends to bleach colour along edges and leaves recesses in shadow. Colour is derived from slips, pinks and oranges resulting where high China clay content (high alumina) is introduced.

I use bicarbonate of soda instead of salt because it is more environmentally friendly and the colour response is softer and brighter. When vaporized, salt gives off a corrosive and potentially hazardous chlorine gas which turns into hydrochloric acid on contact with water vapour.

My work is fired in a gas-fired sprung arch kiln of about 12 cu ft (0.3 cu m) capacity. It is raw-fired to stoneware, cone 10. Test rings are used to check that sufficient soda has been used (usually about 7.7lb, or 3.5kg, of sodium bicarbonate), with a one-hour soak afterwards. Rapid cooling ceases at about 750°C when the kiln is sealed up.

ROBIN WELCH

Eye, Suffolk.
My pots should speak for themselves, and my aim is that each piece should have a 'presence'. From the start, vase and bowl forms have constituted the main part of my one-off work, but experiment has been constant – with quality, with materials, with scale and with form and surface. Large-scale work is a recurrent fascination for me. Composite objects comprising pots, painted plinths and paintings in which the content of each element relates to and complements that of the others are also a recent and continuing development.

Technically, my work is now produced in a multi-firing process. Small forms are simply thrown while larger forms are thrown and added to with further sections, these being either thrown, hand-built, or a combination of the two. I then usually paint or spray white slip on to the form prior to biscuit-firing. All the forms are glazed either wholly or in part and fired in reduction to stoneware temperature. In subsequent firings at lower temperatures, a selection of earthenware glazes, enamels and lustres are used to complete the surface.

DOUG WENSLEY

Papplewick, Nottinghamshire.
For refined, modestly sized sculptural pieces I usually use T-material; more robust structures are built with heavily grogged raku bodies. I have also used fireclay and locally dug brick clays. The latter are cheap and totally unreliable, but they do occasionally produce spectacular eruptions of colour from the unpredictable impurities contained therein. I use integral plinths, resins and cold-cast metals as appropriate to the piece.

I fire to stoneware, cone 8, after biscuiting the pieces, partly to ensure that any weaknesses are identified in the first firing, partly to enable oxides to be applied to the piece without disrupting the surface of the clay. Most are fired in an oxidizing atmosphere in a 5 cu ft (0.14 cu m) top-loading electric kiln ideally suited to my work. For reduction firing I have a twin-burner propane-gas kiln.

My work reflects a preoccupation with eroded forms as found in the landscape, and variations on the human form. It attempts to examine the assumed permanence of form in both medium and manner, these incorporating metamorphosis and change.

JUDITH WENSLEY

Papplewick, Nottinghamshire.
I use the three processes of slabbing, throwing and extruding to produce a range of decorated red earthenware pots within the theme of domestic pottery. One side of the range offers a more traditional approach, while the other is of a more individual variety.

I throw smaller domestic pieces in Potclay's Keuper Red, decorating these by brushing and overlaying stained engobes to achieve subtle variations in the surface. After biscuiting, the pots are glazed with a transparent glaze and fired to 1,100°C with a twenty-minute soak. The soak period gives a mature toasted appearance to the body. Items such as teapots or wonky jars are glazed internally only with honey glaze, but external slipped surfaces are sealed with a weak solution of frit and water, and accentuated with blobs of honey glaze. In this way a variety of contrasts are formed between the rich toasted red of the clay, the smooth sheen of the vitreous fritted engobes, and the fluidity and sparkle of the glazed areas.

Larger pieces (*see* the colour plate captioned 'Jars'; these are 32in, or 82cm, high) are mainly slabbed or extruded using heavily grogged red bodies and are surface treated as above. The larger areas offer a canvas on which greater freedom of expression can be conveyed.

DAVID WHITE

Brier Hey Pottery, Mytholmroyd, West Yorkshire.
My pots are made from clay dug near the pottery and prepared to make a fine red-firing body. Decoration is by majolica technique on a semi-transparent glaze (containing sugar as glaze binder), soaked at 1,120°C to give brown edges from the red clay. The technique could be likened to batik decoration using wax as a means of resisting an overcolour. The colours themselves are mixtures of oxides and prepared ceramic colours, with a little of the glaze and, occasionally, various feldspars to adjust the colour flow or change the colours.

Appendix

TOXIC RAW MATERIALS

Care should be exercised when using and handling the following materials. (**Bold** headings refer to basic materials that are toxic; compounds that contain the basic materials as a constituent are listed after the headings.)

Aluminium Oxide Feldspar, clay.
Antimony Antimony oxide.
Barium Barium carbonate, barium oxide.
Boron Borax (sodium borate), boric acid, calcium borate frit, colemanite.
Cadmium Cadmium compounds.
Calcium oxide Whiting, dolomite.
Chromium Chromium oxide.
Cobalt Cobalt oxide, Cobalt carbonate.
Fluorine Fluorspar (calcium fluoride) traces in minerals. To remove fluorine from the kiln atmosphere, good kiln room ventilation is essential.
Leads, raw Lead carbonate, lead oxide (red lead), lead sulphide (galena), litharge (yellow lead).
Lithium oxide Spodumene, lepidolite.
Magnesium oxide Magnesite, dolomite, talc.
Manganese Manganese compounds (such as manganese dioxide) are also regarded as injurious to health.
Nickel Nickel oxide.
Selenium Selenium compounds.
Silicon Quartz (sand), flint, cristobalite (also present in free silica in most clays).
Sodium oxide Soda feldspar, pearl ash, nitre (soda nitre).
Strontium Strontium oxide, strontium carbonate.
Titanium oxide Rutile.
Vanadium Vanadium pentoxide.
Zinc Zinc oxide.

Hazardous Combinations

While many potters use what are called 'low-solubility lead frits', which by themselves do not present a health hazard, they can become toxic with the addition of certain oxides, such as copper and chromium. This can greatly increase the lead solubility and hence the health risk, especially if acid foods are stored in receptacles glazed in this way. The reason lead frits are still used in glazes is that they give a wide firing range, a low melting range, smoothness and a high gloss. They also give enriching qualities to colours and, if used correctly, are highly acid-resistant.

The compounds of barium, antimony and zinc are also toxic by nature, and most of the basic colouring oxides, such as copper, manganese, cadmium and cobalt, tend to be toxic. Regular mopping up and vacuuming is the best protection against these health hazards. Rubber gloves should be worn when handling soda compounds which are not fritted, and some form of respiratory mask should be worn whenever you are handling powdered glaze materials. If in doubt about any materials, contact the supplier responsible for labelling all the raw materials.

Glossary

Agate ware Made from a stratified mixture of different coloured clays.

Alumina Aluminium oxide (Al_2O_3), highly refractory, reduces drying shrinkage in raw clay.

Bat Highly refractory shelf for kilns; plaster or wooden circular base on which to throw open forms.

Bat wash Protective coating to kiln shelves consisting of two parts alumina hydrate to one part China clay.

Bentonite Primary clay from decomposed volcanic ash which is fine and very plastic. Used to introduce plasticity into clay bodies and aid suspension in glaze mixes; add 2 per cent to bodies and 1 per cent to glazes. As an aid to raw glazing, add up to 10 per cent, thereby replacing China clay.

Bloating Trapped gases in the body cause blistering in stoneware or between slip and body in earthenware.

Blunger Container with mechanized paddle wheels used for preparing mixtures of clay and water as slip.

Borax Hydrated borate of sodium, a chief source of boric acid for glazes. It is soluble in water, so is used in fritted form.

Borax frit A frit made with borax and silica. Used with feldspars and clays to produce leadless glazes.

Brogniart's Principle A formula used to calculate amounts of dry material contained in a liquid:

$$W = \frac{(p-568)}{g-1} \times 9$$

W = dry content (gm) in 1pt water
g = specific gravity. Varies in glazes, but taken as 2.5 for all clays.
p = gram weight of 1pt of liquid

Bung A stack of saggars packed vertically and containing wares requiring protection from direct flame, or to generate local atmospheric conditions within the saggars. Sometimes confused with a vent plug.

Burnishing Rubbing the surface of clay or slip to polish it. Usually makes use of a smooth pebble, spoon or similar tool, causing compression and consolidation of the surface.

Calcine Carbon dioxide and chemical water driven off by subjecting ceramic substances to moderate heat (350–700°C).

Carbon soak Kiln temperature held at about 900°C for thirty minutes or more to facilitate oxidization.

Deflocculan A sodium silicate or sodium carbonate solution. A few drops added to a glaze assists application to vitrified wares, retards settling of glaze and slip, and results in harder setting when dry.

Deflocculation The addition of soluble alkalis called deflocculants to slips and glazes to enable the creation of mixes containing smaller proportions of water. Advantageous in formulating casting slips and glazes capable of adhering to non-porous surfaces.

Dunting Cracks in a pot resulting from stress during firing or cooling, and caused mainly by silica inversions at 226°C and 573°C.

Elephant's ear A natural sponge of fine texture, flattish in shape and about 5in (12.5cm) across. Excellent for press-moulding.

Enamel A soft-melting glass coloured with oxides and used to decorate ceramics, metal and glass. On-glaze enamels are usually used by potters.

Engobe Also vitreous slip. A covering for clay which, like a slip, can be used as a vehicle for oxides. It usually contains glaze materials, will be more vitreous than the body it covers, but does not fire to a glassy state. Being neither simply clay (slip) nor glaze, it applies to any covering mix which falls somewhere between the two.

Faience Colourful decoration or glaze used on earthenware.

Feldspar Also felspar or fieldspar. They contain alumina, silica and alkalis, and are natural frits or glazes.

Fettle To fettle is to trim off excess clay on leather-hard or dry clay, as in removing seam marks from slip-cast pots.

Fireclay Often refractory clay that is associated with coal measures. Used for firebricks. Usually contains volatile impurities.

Firing The process by which clay is changed to pot.

Flashing Coloration and fusion caused by volatiles settling on pots during firing. Considered by some to add interest, but by others as an unwelcome detraction.

Friable Crumbling; easily broken up.

Galena Also lead ore and lead sulphide (PbS). Dangerous source of lead oxide; should not be used.

Grog Refractory material, usually consisting of fired and ground fireclay. Used as filler to open the clay and reduce shrinkage.

High Thermal Insulation (HTI) brick Modern replacement for the less energy efficient refractory brick in kiln linings.

Impressed decoration Decoration pressed or stamped into the clay using wood, metal or biscuit implements.

Inversions – silica Changes to the form of silica giving rise to a sudden expansion or contraction of the body. The processes take place at 225°C and 573°C and are exactly reversible.

Kaolin Also China clay ($Al_2O_3.2SiO_2.2H_2O$). Contains no impurities and is valued for its whiteness, its high alumina content making it highly refractory. Lacks plasticity but is used to introduce silica and alumina to glazes.

Kiss Occurs when two pots become connected in the kiln by fused glaze. After separation, the scars are known as kiss marks.

Kneading Rolling and stretching plastic clay to homogenize it. Usually done on a plaster or concrete wedging bench or slab.

Lead frit Also fritted lead or lead silicate. The most popular is lead bisilicate, widely used in earthenware glazes as a flux with smaller quantities of China clay, feldspar and so on.

Levigation A process which allows heavy particles to settle out while lighter ones remain in suspension in a slip.

Line-blending A practical way of testing requirements for glaze recipes.

Low so Also low solubility. Glazes and frits containing lead oxide with a solubility rating of less than 5 per cent (UK standard).

Lug Projection on a pot that acts as a handle.

Lustre The metallic surface on glazes, involving reduction from compounds to pure metal either applied deliberately or arising accidentally as in raku reduction processes.

Lute Joining two pieces of leather-hard clay by wetting the seam with water for coarser clays and slip for fine bodies.

Marbling The partial blending of two different coloured clays to produce a variegated stain.

Marl Natural red earthenware clays containing high proportions of calcium compounds.

Martin Brothers Pioneers of studio pottery in Britain (1873–1912). They produced salt-glazed stoneware featuring applied decoration, modelling and colouring oxides used with mottled glazes.

Matting agent A ceramic compound added to glazes to give matt surfaces after firing.

Mochaware Decoration applied at the wet-slip stage by a rapid dispersal of alkaline liquid and pigment into the slip.

Muffle Chamber made of refractory material inside a fuel-burning kiln that protects ware from direct contact with gases and flames.

Once-Firing Applying glaze and firing raw pots without an initial biscuit-firing.

Opacifier Used to make glazes opaque. The most widely used is tin oxide, although other oxides can also be used.

Oxidization Kiln atmosphere with an adequate oxygen supply.

Plastic   Malleable; can be modelled and reworked.
Plasticity   Has the capability to be manipulated, retaining its shape as it is modelled.
Porosity   The ability of biscuit ware to absorb moisture.
Primary clay   Clays that remain in their place of origin – for example, China clay.
Pyrometer   Used to record temperatures within a kiln.

Reactive glaze   The softer of two glazes combined by fluxing after application over or under the harder glaze.
Reactive slip   As with most engobes this is fusible, thereby creating a patterned, textured or mottled appearance with its covering glaze.
Reduction   Reduced oxygen supply in a kiln atmosphere which causes changes to the colour of bodies and glazes. The combustion process is effectively reduced to 'stealing' oxygen from compounds contained within the wares, so Fe_2O_3, for example, is reduced to $2FeO$, the O_2 being used up by the fire.
Refractory   Resistant to high temperatures; will not melt at normal ceramic firing temperatures.

Saggar   A fireclay container used to protect ware from flashing when there are no muffles in a kiln.
Salt glaze   Characteristic 'orange peel' surfaced glaze formed by introducing salt into a hot kiln. Not environmentally friendly; *see also* **Sodium glaze**.
Sgraffito   To carve or scratch through a slip to reveal the colour of the clay body beneath.
Shales   Compacted clays, characterized by a flaking tendency.
Silica   Chemical formula SiO_2; is a fundamental oxide of glasses and glazes. Sixty per cent of the Earth's crust consists of silica, so it is usually easy to find and pure. Melts at 1,713°C.
Silk screen   A printing process using stencils supported on a nylon or silk screen.
Slip   Clay with water added to make a creamy paint consistency. Used to coat clay bodies for decorative purposes. Colour can be added in the form of oxides.
Sodium glaze   Using bicarbonate of soda (sodium bicarbonate) instead of salt (sodium chloride) avoids the production of chlorine gas which converts to hydrochloric acid when in contact with a damp atmosphere, causing acid rain.

Terra sigillata   A very fine-grained precipitated slip used as a surface coating prior to burnishing or as a decorative medium.

Underglaze   Oxides modified by the addition of small quantities of glaze (flux) and assisting adhesion to the biscuit-fired body to which they are applied prior to being covered by transparent glaze.

Vent   A small opening in a kiln wall to ventilate the firing chamber, usually circular or square in section. Used to assist adjustment of the atmosphere in the kiln for either oxidization or reduction.
Vent plug   Often referred to as the bung, and used to close or open the vent.
Vitreous slip   Slip containing some flux to enhance the vitrification process.
Vitrification   The point at which a clay body begins to lose its porosity when firing.
Vitrify   Fired successfully to the point where fluxing takes place between the feldspathoids and the free silica in the clay body without deformation. Vitrified wares are virtually non-porous.

Suppliers

Local ceramics suppliers can best be located via their advertisements in periodicals:

UK

Ceramic Review, 21 Carnaby Street, London W1V 1PH.
Studio Pottery, 15 Magdalen Road, Exeter, Devon.
Artists' Newsletter, P.O. Box 23, Sunderland SR4 6DG.
'Crafts' Magazine, Pentonville Road, London N1 9BY.

NORTH AMERICA

American Ceramics, 9 East 45th Street, New York 10017.
Ceramic Arts & Crafts, Livonia, Michigan.
Ceramics Monthly, Box 12448, Columbus, Ohio 43212.
Contact Quarterly, Alberta Potters Association, P.O. Box 1050, Edmonton, Alberta T5J 2M1.
76 Studio Potter Network, 69 High Street, Exeter, New Hampshire 03833.

AUSTRALIA

Craft Australia, Crafts Council of Australia, 27 King Street, Sidney 2000.

FRANCE

La Revue de la Ceramique et du Verre, la Rue Marconi 62880, Vendin Le Vieil, France.

GERMANY

Kevamik Magazin, Rudolf Diesel Stv527, D-50226 Frechen.
Neue Keramik, Unter Den Eichen 90, D-12205 Berlin.

HOLLAND

Kevamiek, Pueldijk 3646, AW Wavereen.

ITALY

Ceramics Italian, Via Firenze 276, 48018 Faenza 276.

NEW ZEALAND

New Zealand Potter, 15 Widestown Road, Wellington 1.

SPAIN

Ceramics, Paseo de las Acacias 9, Madrid 9.

SWEDEN

Form Magazine, Box 7404, S-103 91, Stockholm.

WALES

Crefft, Welsh Arts Council, Museum Place, Cardiff CF1 3NX.

Index